William Blake
Illustrations of the Book of Job

MALCOLM CORMACK

with an Afterword by David Bindman

Virginia Museum of Fine Arts
Richmond

This book was published on the occasion of the exhibition *William Blake: Illustrations of the Book of Job*, November 1, 1997–January 11, 1998. The book and exhibition were made possible by generous gifts from the Paul Mellon Fund, the Lettie Pate Whitehead Evans Exhibitions Fund, and The Council of the Virginia Museum of Fine Arts.

LIBRARY OF CONGRESS CATALOGING-IN-PUBLICATION DATA
Cormack, Malcolm
William Blake: Illustrations of the Book of Job / Malcolm Cormack; with an afterword by David Bindman
p. cm.
Includes bibliographical references and index.
ISBN 0-917046-49-8
1. Blake, William, 1757–1827. Illustrations of the Book of Job. 2. Blake, William, 1757–1827—Criticism and interpretation. I. Blake, William, 1757–1827. Illustrations of the Book of Job. II. Title.
N6797.B57C67 1997
760'.092—DC21 97-29064
CIP

Printed in the United States of America

PHOTOGRAPHY CREDITS

The engraved *Illustrations of the Book of Job*, collection of Virginia Museum of Fine Arts; photographs by Katherine Wetzel, Richmond, Virginia

Watercolors from the Butts set, courtesy of the Pierpont Morgan Library, New York

The portraits of Blake and his preliminary sketches for the *Illustrations of the Book of Job*, courtesy of the Syndics of the Fitzwilliam Museum, Cambridge

The New Zealand set of pencil and watercolor illustrations, courtesy of the Yale Center for British Art, New Haven

COLOPHON
Produced by the Office of Publications, Virginia Museum of Fine Arts, 2800 Grove Avenue, Richmond, VA 23221-2466 USA

Monica S. Rumsey, Editor-in-Chief

Rosalie West, Project Editor

John Hoar, Graphic Designer

Composed by the designer in QuarkXpress

Type set in Adobe Minion

Printed on Mohawk Superfine White Eggshell, 80# text by B&B Printing, Richmond, Virginia

Binding by American Trade Bindery, Inc., Baltimore, Maryland

FRONT COVER: *Job Rebuked by His Friends*, plate 10 of *Illustrations of the Book of Job*, 1825, by William Blake (1757–1827), engraving. Virginia Museum of Fine Arts Purchase, The Arthur and Margaret Glasgow Fund.
BACK COVER: *Job's Evil Dreams*, CA. 1804–7, from a series of Job designs created for Thomas Butts, pen and watercolor. Pierpont Morgan Library, New York, III, 45, Plate 11.

Contents

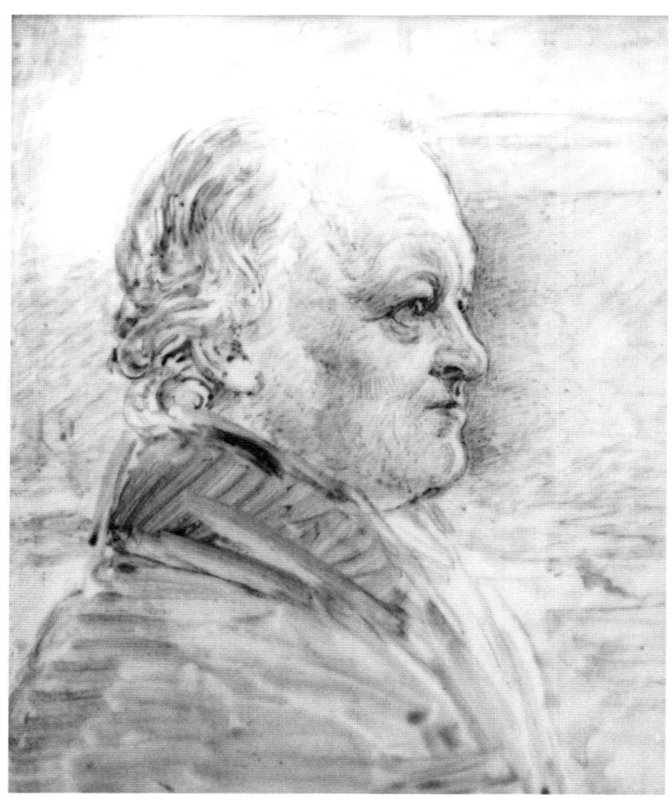

William Blake, 1821, by John Linnell (1792–1882), miniature in watercolor on ivory, 5 1/4 x 4 3/16 inches (133 x 106 MM). Linnell painted this portrait when Blake was beginning his work on the *Illustrations of the Book of Job.* Reproduced by permission of the Syndics of the Fitzwilliam Museum, Cambridge, England.

Foreword

In 1973, the Virginia Museum of Fine Arts acquired William Blake's most important work in the medium of line engraving: a complete set of the *Illustrations of the Book of Job.* Twenty-five years later, we proudly celebrate that acquisition by presenting these remarkable works as the focus of both an exhibition and a book that bring together Blake's *Job* engravings with his preliminary sketches and watercolors. This unique enterprise provides our visitors with the unusual opportunity of viewing Blake's engravings as the product of a long, thoughtful, and intriguing creative process and allows the Museum to display these treasures from its holdings of British art with the elegance and distinction they so richly deserve.

The *Illustrations of the Book of Job* enable us to encounter the character of Job, an enigmatic figure of protest as well as patience with whom Blake closely identified. Job's cry of faith—"Oh that my words were printed in a book that they were graven with an iron pen & lead in the rock forever / for I know that my Redeemer liveth . . ." (JOB 19:23–25)—became Blake's aim in creating these graphic masterpieces.

We are deeply grateful to those who loaned works of art for this exciting project: New York's Pierpont Morgan Library; the Yale Center for British Art, New Haven, Connecticut; and the Fitzwilliam Museum, Cambridge, England. We also owe our thanks to the donors of the Virginia Museum's Arthur and Margaret Glasgow Fund, which permitted the original purchase of Blake's engravings. Finally, we appreciate the generosity of Paul Mellon, who has continued to support the acquisition, display, and publication of British painting, prints, and sculpture at the Virginia Museum of Fine Arts, and whose fund at the Virginia Museum of Fine Arts has made the publication of this book possible.

KATHARINE C. LEE
Director
Virginia Museum of Fine Arts

Preface

The English artist and poet William Blake (1757–1827) has been the subject of innumerable publications in the twentieth century, to which this present catalogue modestly adds one more. Yet in his own lifetime Blake was ignored, except by a few devoted patrons and admirers; his first biographer, Alexander Gilchrist (1863), called him "Pictor Ignotus" (the unknown artist). He seems to embody all that we now think of as a misunderstood romantic genius, poor but dedicated to his art. He was, perhaps, better known as a writer and engraver rather than as a painter. According to the diarist Crabb Robinson, William Wordsworth remarked in 1812 that "there was no doubt that this poor man was mad, but there is something in the madness of this man which interests me more than the sanity of Lord Byron and Walter Scott." Blake was eccentric, and his profound and individual views of art, literature, and religion were not easily accepted.

Blake's Life and Art

Blake's own activities did nothing to help his career. He was anti-establishment, conducted a vendetta against the venerated president of the Royal Academy, Sir Joshua Reynolds, and was even charged with sedition: "D-n the King, d-n all his subjects," he is reported as saying as he ejected a soldier from his garden at Felpham. He knew Thomas Paine and other republican sympathizers such as the publisher Joseph Johnson. His religious views were as individual as his artistic attitudes: he considered himself a Christian, and was influenced to some extent by the ideas of the Swedish philosopher Emmanuel Swedenborg, yet ultimately he did not adhere to the tenets of either the Church of England or Swedenborg's New Church. He also denied the principles of the Age of Reason; he was against the rationality of Locke and Newton and declared that the earth was flat. In this regard he was, undoubtedly, a member of that amorphous body of ideas that constitute the Romantic movement.

Blake's art was complicated by its integration with his writing; unlike most writers, he designed his own poetry and prophetic books with a laborious combination of illustration and text. Would his writings have been more acceptable to the public if they had not been surrounded by strange imagery? Would his figurative art—which, after all, dealt with the traditional values of "the Human Form Divine"—have been better appreciated if his godlike creatures had been named Venus, Jupiter, Athena, or Apollo instead of Oothoon, Rintrah, Enion, or Los? His unique combination of recondite narratives and dense, distorted images, executed with surprisingly revolutionary techniques, were difficult to assimilate.

In Blake's prophetic book *Jerusalem* the poet-prophet Los declares, "I must create a system or be enslav'd by another Man's." This credo was to be the basis of much of Blake's art, but, as with other Romantic artists, he did not overthrow all other art or all other writings. In his eclecticism he can be compared to Neoclassical artists such as Jacques-Louis David and John Flaxman, who was a fellow student and friend. Blake extolled the virtues of Raphael, Dürer, and Michelangelo, as did his friend and admirer, the artist Henry Fuseli. Blake's own images, based as they often were on engravings after other artists, proposed an art of line and contour, rather than color or an examination of nature expressed with painterly values. He was thus set apart from those other giants of the Romantic movement, such as J. M.W. Turner, Eugène Delacroix, and John Constable. When shown a drawing of trees in Constable's studio he is reported as saying, "But that is inspiration," to which Constable laconically replied, "I thought it was merely drawing."

Blake's Influence

The influence of Blake's art finally became apparent in the mid nineteenth century with Pre-Raphaelite artist Dante Gabriel Rossetti, who also interlinked art and poetry, and William Morris, whose combined interest in ancient sagas and medieval design is a further example of Blake's legacy. From the point of view of design, the art of Blake transcended the Romantic movement and looked forward both to the curvilinear shapes of Art Nouveau and to the emphasis on individual imagination characteristic of the group called *Der Blaue Reiter* in Germany (where there had always been some sympathy for his work). Their prospectus of 1911 stated, "We seek today, behind the veil of external appearances, the hidden things which seem to us more important than the discoveries of the Impressionists—we search out and elaborate this spiritual side of ourselves in nature. . . ."

More recently, the poetry and designs of the Welsh poet David Jones (1895–1974) continued Blake's combination of word and image, while the ethos of the 1960s, especially through the poetry and enthusiasms of Alan Ginsberg, further championed Blake's endeavor. The psychological analyses of Freud and Jung and the art of the Surrealists revived interest in Blake and encouraged symbolic interpretation of his art.

Blake and the *Book of Job*

Blake's interest in the biblical *Book of Job* dated from early in his career, and he illustrated it according to his own religious theories, drawing upon the Judeo-Christian tradition and his unique spritual vision.

Written about 500–400 B.C. and considered part of the Old Testament, the *Book of Job* is a powerful extended poem or parable that explores the perennial religious question of "undeserved suffering": why people of good behavior and fervent faith should suffer great affliction and sorrow. Everyone in the narrative—even God—agrees that Job was "perfect and upright... and eschewed evil" (JOB 1:1), and yet God allows Satan to deprive him of everything: his children and servants, his livestock and his house. As a final blow, Satan "smote Job with sore boils from the sole of his foot unto his crown" (JOB 2:7). Although at first Job accepts these disasters as the will of God (hence the popular notion of "the patience of Job"), this patience soon gives way to an impassioned protest against the way he has been treated and his resulting sense of isolation from God. In a series of dialogues with Job, his three friends—Eliphaz, Bildad, and Zophar—alternately comfort him and accuse him of deserving his punishment; in a fourth dialogue, the young man Elihu even accuses Job of thinking his "righteousness is more than God's" (JOB 35:2). Despite these challenges, Job maintains both his innocence and his belief in God's goodness as he explores his own nature and the nature of God. Although Job never finds a satisfactory reason for his suffering, God does reveal himself to Job "out of the whirlwind," thus establishing His omnipotence and reestablishing their relationship. Job accepts that God "canst do everything" and repents "in dust and ashes" (JOB 42:2, 6). After he and his friends make the appropriate sacrifices to God, Job receives back more than he had lost, including more children: "So the Lord blessed the latter end of Job more than the beginning" (JOB 42:12).

Very early on, Christians developed a typological view of the Old Testament, that is, they saw the people and events described therein as prefiguring or symbolizing similar elements in the New Testament. Job, in enduring great loss and then being restored to good fortune, was seen to prefigure Christ's suffering and redemption. As Bo Lindberg (1973) pointed out, the Lord's Prayer is inscribed on the very first illustration of Job, with a Gothic cathedral in the background, which suggests a Christian interpretation. Blake presents Job as fallen and resurrected man, a Protestant everyman who could make his own resurrection.

This was not enough for Blake. With his diligent reading of the Bible (the King James or "Authorized Version"), and his own belief in the power of imagination, he could express in his *Illustrations of the Book of Job* the summation of his artistic and religious ideals. On a simple level, he has provided a series of images which illustrate the story as if they were early engravings after a series of wall frescoes in a church. Yet these images do not follow entirely the sequence of events as narrated in the Authorized Version of the Bible. Blake added scenes that do not tally with the text. For example, he shows Job seeing not only God but also Satan. He has also included a mixture of texts from the Old and New Testaments—both the King James Version and the Vulgate, including the Apocrypha—which add literary as well as visual layers of meaning. The commentary accompanying the individual plates explains these additions.

Blake's saddened view of Christianity in his own times, with its "Stony Laws of Moses" (expressed in Blake's *The Marriage of Heaven and Hell*), or the "Yea, nay creeping Jesus," as he put it in a letter to his friend George Cumberland, are all part of his interpretation of the *Book of Job*. In the end, imagination and forgiveness were to Blake religious virtues. Man was a cog in the dreadful, increasing materialism of the industrial revolution. Job was similarly caught in the world of laws and rationality, but was finally freed by his belief in the spiritual and artistic nature of salvation. These ideas transcend the ages, and as the musical instruments are brought down from the trees in the final image, they give us hope.

MALCOLM CORMACK
Paul Mellon Curator
Virginia Museum of Fine Arts

Acknowledgments

I wish, first of all, to acknowledge a debt to the enthusiasm of Professor David Bindman, who carried me all those years ago in Cambridge to a better understanding of Blake. His essay is an important part of this catalogue. In Cambridge, I profited from the presence of Sir Geoffrey Keynes and the friendship and writings of Martin Butlin. Bo Lindberg's work has been especially valuable. I must also thank Dr. Charles E. Pierce, Jr., Director, and Stephanie Wiles, Curator of Drawings and Prints, at the Pierpont Morgan Library, in New York; my previous colleague, Patrick Noon, then Curator of Prints and Drawings at the Yale Center for British Art; and my successors at the Fitzwilliam Museum, Cambridge. Finally I am indebted to the present director of the Fitzwilliam, Duncan Robinson; the Keeper of Paintings and Drawings, David Scrase; and the senior Assistant Keeper, Jane Munro, for the facilitation of loans and much help besides.

Nearer at hand, I am grateful for the invaluable assistance of intern Claire Black and the indefatigable transcriptions of Diana Dougherty in the Virginia Museum's Collections Division. Eileen Mott, educational advisor for both this publication and the exhibition, worked vigilantly to help both readers and visitors become comfortably oriented in Blake's world. In the Publications Department of the Museum, led by Monica Rumsey, editor Rosalie West and designer John Hoar shaped a dense text to provide, as always, a handsome publication, which has further benefited from the advice of Chief Graphic Designer Sarah Lavicka and the elegant photography of Katherine Wetzel. The staff of the Museum Library, led by Suzanne Freeman, were assiduous in acquiring books through interlibrary loans, not the least of which was the acquisition of a remaining copy of the Blake Trust Edition of Blake's *Illustrations of the Book of Job.* The design of the accompanying exhibition was entrusted to Tom Baker, ably assisted by the display graphics staff: Kathy DeHaven, Michelle Edmonds, and Kent Lovelace. Richard Woodward and Carol Moon in the Exhibitions and Planning Division made sure that the installation of the exhibit was handled with ease, that the labels and wall texts were both accurate and accessible, and that all contracts were as straightforward as Linnell's with Blake. Lisa Hancock, Chief Registrar; Mary Sullivan, Registration Information Analyst; and Art Handlers Andrew Kovach, Frank Milik, Roy Thompson, and Randy Wilkinson ensured that Blake's admonitions against the rules of law were taken in the best interests of his work.

Finally, I must acknowledge the advice of Professor Robert McCubbin of the College of William and Mary, Williamsburg, Virginia, and the assistance of Ronald Epps of the Virginia Museum's Education and Outreach Division in organizing a symposium, in which, it is hoped, "the Lord blessed the latter end of Job more than the beginning."

M.C.

William Blake: Chronology

1757 Born November 28 at 28 Broad Street, Soho, London. Baptized December 11 at St. James's, Piccadilly.
Blake was the third of five children born to James Blake, a hosier, and Catherine Blake. He did not attend school but was educated at home, primarily by his mother.

1767 Aged 10, entered William Shipley's Academy in the Strand, a drawing school continued by Henry Pars after 1768.
It was the school's mission "to introduce Boys and Girls of Genius to Masters and Mistresses in such manufactories as require Fancy and ornament, and for which the knowledge of Drawing is absolutely necessary. . . ." He studied basic draftsmanship and some time later made drawings of plaster casts of antique sculptures in the Duke of Richmond's collection in Whitehall. In addition, his father purchased three casts, presumably on a small scale; at this young age he would not have been allowed to work from live models.

The ten-year-old Blake had probably already begun collecting prints by Raphael (probably reproductive prints after Raphael by Marcantonio Raimondi), Michelangelo, Martin van Heemskerck, Dürer, and Giulio Romano. He later wrote, "I am happy I cannot say that Rafael Ever was from my Earliest Childhood hidden from me." From his beginning as an artist, Blake was interested in the hard outlined prints of Dürer and those aspects of High Renaissance and Mannerist art that emphasized the human figure in complicated poses.

1768 Foundation of Royal Academy, with Sir Joshua Reynolds (1732–1762) as its first president.

1772 Aged 14, apprenticed to line engraver James Basire (1730–1802) for the large sum of 50 guineas, paid by his father.
Thus began Blake's lifelong concern with the engraver's craft, which emphasized the strong outlines found in all of Blake's art, especially his *Illustrations of the Book of Job.*

Basire sent Blake to Westminster Abbey to make drawings of its Gothic monuments for the publication of Richard Gough's *Sepulchral Monuments in Great Britain* (1786). Given the assignment to reproduce monochromatic sculpture, Blake imbibed the skills of line engraving and etching: grinding and smoothing the copper plate; engraving the image on the plate with a graver or etching needle; inking the plate; and pressing the finished image on paper. Blake had no desire to experiment with the "softer" methods of mezzotint, which were fashionable in the late eighteenth century as a means of reproducing the subtleties of chiaroscuro (light and shadow) in contemporary oil painting. "All depends on form and outline," he was to write in 1809.

Basire's studio provided the basis for Blake's attitudes toward art, but it also put him into the lowly class of copy engraver. Blake's prolonged study of the Gothic style in sculpture and architecture later influenced his imaginative and eclectic style. His early exposure to Gothic monuments also brought about a lifelong fascination for the medieval past, an aspect of Romanticism that was to lead to the Gothic revivalism of the nineteenth century.

1773 Engraved his earliest known picture, *Joseph of Arimathea Among the Rocks of Albion* (based on a figure in Michelangelo's *Crucifixion of St. Peter*).
This engraving was a significant and early attempt by Blake to turn the musculature of Michelangelo's image into his private vision of the introduction of Christianity into England (Albion). This eclectic use of the art of other periods and countries (learned through engravings, since he never went abroad) characterized his art throughout his career.

1779 Admitted to the Royal Academy Schools as an engraver, the lowest in the hierarchy; fellow students were John Flaxman (1756–1826), Thomas Stothard (1755–1834), and George Cumberland (1754–1848).
Blake, Flaxman, Stothard, and Cumberland were all interested in book illustration, of which Blake's *Illustrations of the Book of Job* is one example. These artists all became significant in the development of the Neoclassical and Romantic movements, not only for their expressive linear technique, but also for their interest in the art of other cultures that were not then considered part of normal Academic training; for example, Flaxman and Blake were early admirers of Indian art, and Persian and Mughal miniatures.

Sir Joshua Reynolds's *Discourses* to the students at the Academy staunchly defended an ideal, rational view of history painting in the "grand manner," a position antipathetic to Blake's personal vision of art. Blake later conducted a vendetta against Reynolds, writing in the margin of his copy of the *Discourses*, "This Man was Hired to Depress Art." Ironically, however, Blake's figurative work expressed some of the ideas of history painting that Reynolds had attempted to uphold.

Blake lasted one year as a student at the Royal Academy. Though there are some early studies, he was not interested in drawing from plaster casts or, eventually, proceeding to live models, which was the course presented by the Academy. During his career, he was very rarely to draw from life, relying instead upon the strength of his imagination for his figurative style.

1780 Exhibited an historical design in watercolor at the Royal Academy, *The Death of the Earl of Godwin.*

1782 Married Catherine Butcher (or Boucher) (1762–1831), illiterate daughter of a market-gardener; they had no children.

In the early years of the marriage, Blake taught his wife not only to read and write, but also to draw, to prepare his colors, and to make impressions of his engravings. Theirs was a long and exclusive relationship, with Catherine assuming the role of wife, supporter, protector, and helpmate.

1783 Publication of his collection of early *Poetical Sketches* (written 1769–78), financed with the help of Flaxman and Rev. and Mrs. A. S. Matthews.

Rev. Matthews and his wife conducted salon evenings at which Blake was known to have sung his poems to melodies that he composed himself, a practice that he continued throughout his life.

1784 Exhibited a number of historical designs at the Royal Academy: for example, *War Unchained by an Angel, Fire and Pestilence and Famine Following,* and *A Breach in a City Wall.*

Blake's fervent and gloomy view of mankind, which he redeems through his interpretation of the *Book of Job*, is already apparent.

Death of Blake's father, James, who left Blake a small inheritance with which he opened a print shop in partnership with James Parker (1705–1805).

In London, at the turn of the century, print selling had developed into a lucrative profession, and it appears that Blake's shop both made and sold prints. The wooden press that Blake purchased for the shop was to prove invaluable to him in later years, allowing him the freedom of experimentation with his own works. The partnership did not last long.

Blake's dependence upon—and his attempts to be independent from—the print trade were already apparent. His illuminated books, which were designed, set up, printed (sometimes enhanced with watercolor, and arranged with the aid of his wife), were sold as orders came in. His engraved plates for the *Book of Job* were actually printed by a professional printer, but sets were still made on demand.

1785 Exhibited at the Royal Academy three large watercolors of the *Story of Joseph* from the Bible and *The Bard* from Thomas Gray. Made first drawings connected with the subject of Job.

CIRCA 1785–6 First unique state of line engraving of Job, without title.

1787 Death of Robert Blake, William's younger brother.

For the rest of his life, Blake had a close, spiritual relationship with Robert. "I converse daily & hourly in the Spirit & See him in my remembrance in the regions of my Imagination. I hear his advice & even now write from his Dictate."

Studied the works of Swedish philosopher and religious writer Emmanuel Swedenborg (1688-1772).

Blake discovered in the Swedenborgian New Jerusalem Church a philosophy that supported his own unconventional beliefs—in the reality of angels and spirits, and in the material forms of this world, which each contain a celestial, spiritual, and natural sense. Thus, Blake would later write of "eternity in a grain of sand."

1787–88 Experimented with first works of illuminated printing: *All Religions Are One* and *There Is No Natural Religion.* Probably began drawings for *Tiriel,* one of his first prophetic books. Began associating with the radical circle of Mary Wollstonecraft, William Godwin, Joseph Priestley, Thomas Paine, and Joseph Johnson. Met the painter Henry Fuseli (Johann Heinrich Füssli, 1741–1825), with whom he had some spiritual affinity.

According to an unpublished biography of Blake by Frederick Tatham (1805–1878), "Blake was more fond of Fuseli than any other man on earth." Fuseli, on the other hand, stated that "Blake was damned good to steal from," which perhaps gives some measure of their relationship. Blake, however, also "borrowed" from Fuseli.

Both Fuseli and Blake deeply admired Raphael and Michelangelo, and their images reflected a romantic reinterpretation of sixteenth-century Italian art, but whereas Fuseli's writings on art were quite conventional, as was his later career (he was elected to the Royal Academy in 1790, and in 1799 became Professor of Painting at the Academy), Blake's writings were deeply personal, and he never gained professional recognition.

1789 Published his own illuminated books: *The Book of Thel* and *Songs of Innocence.* Blake and his wife signed articles of belief at the Swedenborgian New Jerusalem Church but never actually became members.
Songs of Innocence, Blake's best-known work, of which twenty-one copies of the original edition exist, was published at a time when the popularity of children's literature was flourishing in England (*Mother Goose* was already well known).

1790 Moved to Lambeth, an area of London south of the Thames. Supported the French Revolution. Began work on *The Marriage of Heaven and Hell*, a satirical view of Swedenborg's ideas of an institutionalized religion, which is part of his interpretation of the *Book of Job.*
For Blake and his wife, the years spent at Lambeth were productive, but not prosperous. From then on, Blake was involved with writing, designing, printing, and publishing his own works. *The Marriage of Heaven and Hell* was a strange mixture of prophetic verse and proverbs, containing some of Blake's most powerful epigrams and showing his divergence from the teachings of Swedenborg.

1791 Published his poem *The French Revolution* for the bookseller Joseph Johnson.

1793 Second state of engraving of Job, entitled *Job* and inscribed: *Job / What Is Man That Thou Shouldst Try Him Every Moment.* Paired with *Ezekial* (dated 1794; first unique state, untitled, dated about 1785–6).

1794 Publication of the illuminated books *Songs of Experience, Europe*, and *The Book of Urizen.*
Blake was not only producing poetry, with an individual and moving voice, but he was also engaged in complicated methods of relief etching for his poetry and prophetic books. This laborious printing method entailed engraving both illustration and lettering on one plate, rather than engraving illustrations separately from the text. Blake's books were completely his own creations; he was responsible for the engraving, the printing, and the hand-coloring, making each book a unique and individual work.

1795 Created *The Song of Los, The Book of Ahania*, and *The Book of Los.* Began a series of twelve colored monotypes, including the well-known *Newton* and *Nebuchadnezzar.* Commissioned by Richard Edwards to illustrate Edward Young's *Night Thoughts.*
Originally, Blake completed 537 watercolor drawings for *Night Thoughts*, but the final edition, of which 20 deluxe copies were printed in 1797, contained only 43 engravings. This was an example of Blake adding his illustrations to a printed text by another writer. With *Job* and other of his illustrated books, both text and design are fully integrated.

1796 Engraved eight plates for George Cumberland's publication *Thoughts on Outline.* Began work on *Vala or The Four Zoas*, his first long poem. Began a descent into poverty.
Vala was revised over the years as *The Four Zoas*, and eventually abandoned in manuscript form. After the relative failure of *Night Thoughts*, Blake fell out of favor as a commercial engraver. His pessimistic outlook was reflected in one of his notebooks: "I say I shan't live five years. And if I live one, it will be a Wonder."

1797 Commissioned by John Flaxman to illustrate Thomas Gray's *Poems* (completed in 1798).
Flaxman commissioned this work as a gift to his wife. The lighter qualities of Gray's poetry, after the rigors of *Night Thoughts*, appealed to Blake; the illustrations for this text are strong yet charming in their lightness and humor.

1799 Received first commissions from Thomas Butts. Exhibited his first "tempera" painting, *The Last Supper*, at the Royal Academy.
Thomas Butts (1757–1845), a clerk in the office of the Muster-Master General, was to become Blake's constant and faithful patron, commissioning and purchasing over a hundred religious watercolors (for which he paid one guinea each) and fifty paintings in Blake's "tempera" technique. Blake's unusual technique, which he called "tempera" or "fresco," involved a canvas backing, a ground of whiting, carpenter's glue as a medium with watercolor, and linear details added in pen and ink. These materials absorbed moisture, which often caused lifting and darkening.

1799–1800 Probable date of "tempera" painting of *Job and His Daughters.* Exhibited a "tempera" painting of *The Loaves and the Fishes* at the Royal Academy.

1800 Moved to Felpham (Sussex), on the south coast of England near Chichester, to work for William Hayley (1745–1820), a minor poet. Studied Latin, Greek, and Hebrew.
For three years (1800–1803), William Hayley supported Blake's work, commissioning such works as the *Heads of the Poets* (eighteen tempera paintings) and Blake's only series of miniatures. Temperamentally, however, the patron and painter were incompatible. Finally, in 1803, Blake returned to London and wrote of Hayley "As a Poet he is frighten'd at me & as a Painter his views & mine are

opposite; he thinks to turn me into a Portrait Painter, . . . but this he nor all the devils in hell will never do." His letters to Hayley, however, were always polite and grateful.

1801 Commissioned by Rev. J. Thomas to illustrate Milton's *Comus* and Shakespeare.

1802 Illustrated Hayley's *Ballads.*

1803 Engraved four plates for Hayley's *Life of William Cowper* and six plates after Maria Flaxman for Hayley's *Triumphs of Temper.* Charged with sedition after ejecting a soldier from his garden in Felpham. Returned to London.

1804 Possible date for beginning of watercolors of Job for Thomas Butts. Dated title pages for *Milton, a Poem* and *Jerusalem, the Emanation of the Giant Albion.* Acquitted of sedition charge.
Blake's former patron, William Hayley, supported the artist's claim of innocence and was instrumental in having the sedition charges acquitted.

1805 Hayley's *Ballads* reissued with Blake's illustrations. Commissioned by Robert Hartley Cromek to illustrate Robert Blair's poem, *The Grave.*
This commission eventually resulted in extremely shabby treatment of Blake by Cromek, who reneged on his agreement and, while accepting Blake's designs, gave most of the lucrative engraving work to Louis Schiavionetti. Blake used proof sheets of Hayley's *Ballads* as wrappers for his preliminary drawings for the *Book of Job,* now in the Fitzwilliam Museum.

1806 Publication of Benjamin Heath Malkin's *A Father's Memoirs of His Child,* which contains the earliest account of Blake's career and originally included an engraving by Cromeck after Blake for its frontispiece.

1807 Executed first set of illustrations for Milton's *Paradise Lost* for Rev. Joseph Thomas. Portrait of Blake by Thomas Phillips exhibited at Royal Academy.

1808 Exhibited two watercolors at Royal Academy: *Jacob's Dream* and *Christ in the Sepulchre.* Produced a second monumental set of watercolors illustrating Milton's *Paradise Lost.* Designs for *The Grave* attacked by Robert Hunt in *The Examiner.*
Hunt described Blake's designs as "absurd." Another critic, writing in the *Anti-Jacobin,* described them as "the offspring of a morbid fancy."

1809 Blake's exhibition, with his own *Descriptive Catalogue of Pictures: Poetical and Historical Inventions,* opened in the house where he was born at 28 Broad St., now occupied by his brother James. Blake's work again attacked in *The Examiner* by Robert Hunt.
Blake opened an exhibition of sixteen of his paintings, mostly "temperas," including the *Chaucer's Canterbury Pilgrims,* which Stothard had also chosen to design. In his catalogue, Blake sought to justify his aims: "The eye that can prefer the colouring of Titian and Rubens to that of Michael Angelo and Rafael, ought to be modest and to doubt its own powers. . . . Mr. B. Appeals to the Public, from the Judgement of those narrow blinking eyes, that have too long governed art in a dark corner . . . all depends on Form or Outline. . . . We never shall equal Rafael and Albert Dürer, Michael Angelo, and Julio Romano. . . . Clearness and precision have been the chief object in painting these Pictures. . . ."

Hunt described Blake as "an unfortunate lunatic whose personal inoffensiveness secures him from confinement," whose catalogue contained "the wild ebullitions of a distempered brain." The exhibition was a complete failure.

1810–18 Nadir of Blake's career from an economic point of view. Completed watercolors for a proposed edition of Milton's *Paradise Regained* and engravings for *Jerusalem, the Emanation of the Giant Albion.*

1810 Began work on engraving after his painting *Chaucer's Canterbury Pilgrims,* which was included in his exhibition. The exhibition continued on into the early summer, when Crabb Robinson visited it.
At the same time that Blake was working on his engraving of the *Canterbury Pilgrims,* he composed, in his notebook, a series of writings entitled "Chaucer's Canterbury Pilgrims Being a Complete Index of Human Characters as they appear Age after Age." The thoughts in this collection eventually veered away from Chaucer and became a lengthy treatise by Blake on the commercialization and industrialization of society, which would eventually transform the practice of art. He allowed himself a lengthy diatribe against what he thought was false in art, which he published in his *Descriptive Catalogue:* "As there is a class of men whose whole delight is the destruction of men, so there is a class of artists, whose whole art and science is fabricated for the purposes of destroying art. Who these are is soon known: 'by their works ye shall know them.' All who endeavour to raise up a style against Rafael, Mich. Angelo, and the Antique; those who separate

Painting from Drawing; who look if a picture is well Drawn, and if it is, immediately cry out, that it cannot be well Coloured—those are the men."

1811 Publication of Henry Crabb Robinson's essay, "William Blake, Künstler, Dichter und Religiöser Schwärmer" (Artist, Poet and Religious Visionary) in Hamburg.

Robinson (1775–1867) was a lawyer and an admirer of German art, Goethe, and the art of William Blake. His diaries (first published in 1869) contain lengthy records of the English literary scene at the beginning of the nineteenth century (he was a friend of the poets William Wordsworth and Samuel Taylor Coleridge and the essayists Charles Lamb and William Hazlett). His essay on Blake gave an important notice to young German artists of the Romantic period about Blake's work and art. He later procured subscriptions for Blake's *Illustrations of the Book of Job*, and his diaries record that Blake "spoke of his being richer than ever having learned to know me."

1812 Exhibited at the Associated Painters in Water Color: *The Canterbury Pilgrims, The Spiritual Form of Pitt Guiding Behemoth, The Spiritual Form of Nelson Guiding Leviathan,* and *Detached Specimen of an Original Illuminated Poem, Entitled "Jerusalem, the Emanation of the Giant Albion."*

1814 Blake's fellow student and a long-suffering supporter, George Cumberland, remarked that Blake was "still poor still Dirty." A year later, his two sons found Blake and his wife "drinking Tea durtyer [sic] than ever.... His time is now intirely [sic] taken up with Etching and Engraving."

While some of his time was through necessity dedicated to making commercial engravings (such as the outlines of Wedgwood ware for pattern-books), Blake continued to pursue his artistic vision. His beautiful watercolors for an unpublished edition of Milton's *Paradise Regained* advanced his ideas of the relationship between God and Satan, expressed in his *Illustrations of the Book of Job.* For his epic poem *Jerusalem, the Emanation of the Giant Albion,* he engraved over a hundred illustrations.

1818 *Songs of Innocence and of Experience* praised by poet Samuel Taylor Coleridge. Met three painters: John Linnell (1792–1882), John Varley (1778–1842), and John Constable (1776–1837).

Coleridge was given a copy of *Songs of Innocence and Experience* by Charles Augustus Tulk, a noted Swedenborgian who was also a friend of John Flaxman. Coleridge remarked that Blake "is a man of Genius, and I apprehend, a Swedenborgian. Certainly, a mystic *emphatically.*"

Blake's friendship with Linnell was extremely important; it was Linnell who was to suggest the engraving of the *Illustrations of the Book of Job.* Young John Varley became an energetic, high-spirited disciple of Blake who believed in astrology, clairvoyance, and, quite firmly, in Blake's mystical visions. Blake's drawings of "visionary heads" were based on visions of historical figures that came to him during nighttime seances with Varley.

1821 Publication by Dr. Robert John Thornton of *The Pastorals of Virgil,* which contained four wood engravings and seventeen woodcuts by Blake.

For this schoolboy's edition of Virgil, Ambrose Philips supplied an imitation of *Eclogue I* set in Britain with an ancient British hero and heroine, and Blake created the illustrations. Although Blake's wood engravings and woodcuts did not satisfy Thornton, they were to provide inspiration to "The Ancients," a young artistic group of Blake admirers and imitators, led by Samuel Palmer (SEE BELOW, ENTRY FOR 1825).

Sold print collection; moved to 3 Fountain Court, off the Strand, the address on the label of Blake's *Illustrations of the Book of Job.*

Blake and his wife were so destitute that he was forced to sell the print collection that he had amassed since childhood to Colnaghi, a London art dealer, holding on only to his copy of Dürer's *Melancholia.* The painter Samuel Palmer remarked about Blake that "he ennobled poverty, and, by his conversation and the influence of his genius, made two small rooms in Fountain Court more attractive than the threshold of princes."

Began preliminary work on *Illustrations of the Book of Job.*

1822 Received a donation from the Royal Academy Council.

Because of his continuing hardships, the Royal Academy paid Blake, "an able Designer & Engraver laboring under great distress," the sum of twenty-five pounds. Blake produced a short illustrated verse drama, *The Ghost of Abel, A Revelation in the Visions of Jehovah Seen by William Blake.*

1823 Agreement with Linnell to engrave *Illustrations of the Book of Job.* James Deville made a life mask of Blake, now in the Fitzwilliam Museum, Cambridge.

In March, Blake and Linnell signed a Memorandum of Agreement for Blake to engrave and Linnell to publish the engravings of the *Book of Job*. Blake produced a set of small-scale sketches (mostly in pencil with some colored wash) for the twenty-one scenes actually engraved.

1824 Commissioned by Linnell to engrave illustrations for Dante's *Divine Comedy*; executed a series of watercolors illustrating *The Pilgrim's Progress*; began series illustrating the *Book of Genesis*.

Linnell continued his support of Blake by commissioning a series of drawings illustrating Dante's *Divine Comedy*, which were meant to be engraved later. Only seven of the engravings were ever made, but more than a hundred watercolors remain as a testament to Blake's remarkable imaginative sense of design and color. Blake visited Linnell in Hampstead.

1825 Completed two tempera paintings: *The Black Madonna* and *The Characters of Spenser's Faerie Queene*; worked on overseeing final proofs for the *Illustrations for the Book of Job*; met members of the group called "The Ancients."

In October, Blake took a copy of *Job* to John Flaxman, who admired it and bought a copy. Blake met Charles (Karl) Aders (1780–1846), a partner in an Anglo-German import-export firm and an important pioneer collector of Northern Medieval and early Renaissance art. Aders is recorded as purchasing a proof set of the *Job* engravings for five guineas in July, 1826. He also owned a copy of *The Songs of Innocence*.

"The Ancients," whose catchphrase was "Poetry and Sentiment," were a group of young artists headed by the visionary landscape artist Samuel Palmer (1805–1881). They believed for a time that ancient man far superseded contemporary man, and they found inspiration in the work of William Blake, considering him both guide and sage.

1826 Publication of *The Illustrations of the Book of Job* (dated 1825).

Blake's health began to deteriorate severely. Two watercolors, *The Wise and Foolish Virgins* and *Queen Catherine's Dream*, sold to Sir Thomas Lawrence.

1827 Severe illness persisted. Blake continued work on Dante engravings and a colored print of *The Ancient of Days*; died on August 12 at Fountain Court.

In April, Blake wrote a long letter to his friend George Cumberland which included a list of works available for sale and a moving description of his own condition: "I have been very near the Gates of Death and have returned very weak & am an old man feeble and tottering, but not in Spirit & Life, not in The Real Man The Imagination which Liveth for Ever. In that I am stronger & stronger as this Foolish Body decays. I thank you for the Pains you have taken with Poor Job. . . ."

About Blake's death, his friend George Richmond wrote "He said He was going to that Country he had all His life wished to see & expressed Himself Happy hoping for Salvation through Jesus Christ." Blake's funeral was attended by only his wife and several friends; he was buried in an unmarked common grave in Bunhill Fields Burial Ground. Catherine Blake went to live with Linnell at Circencester Place, as his housekeeper.

1828 Catherine Blake moved to 20 Lisson Grove as Frederick Tatham's housekeeper.

1830 Publication of Allan Cunningham's *Lives of the Most Eminent British Painters, Sculptors and Architects*, with a long section on Blake.

1831 Death of Catherine Blake, on October 18.

Blake's Watercolors of the *Book of Job* from the Butts Set

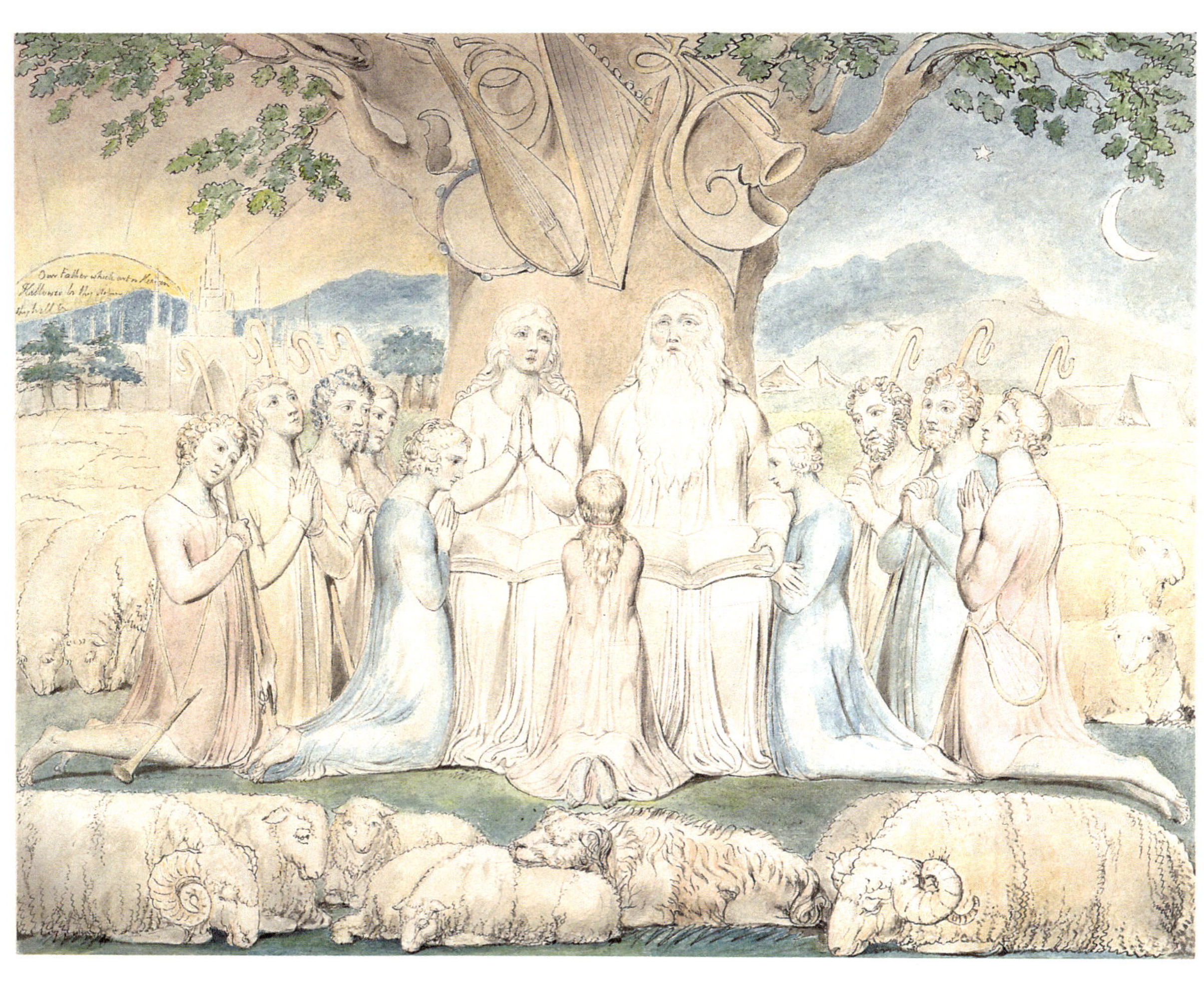

COLOR PLATE I **JOB AND HIS FAMILY** SEE NO. 1A, PAGE 21

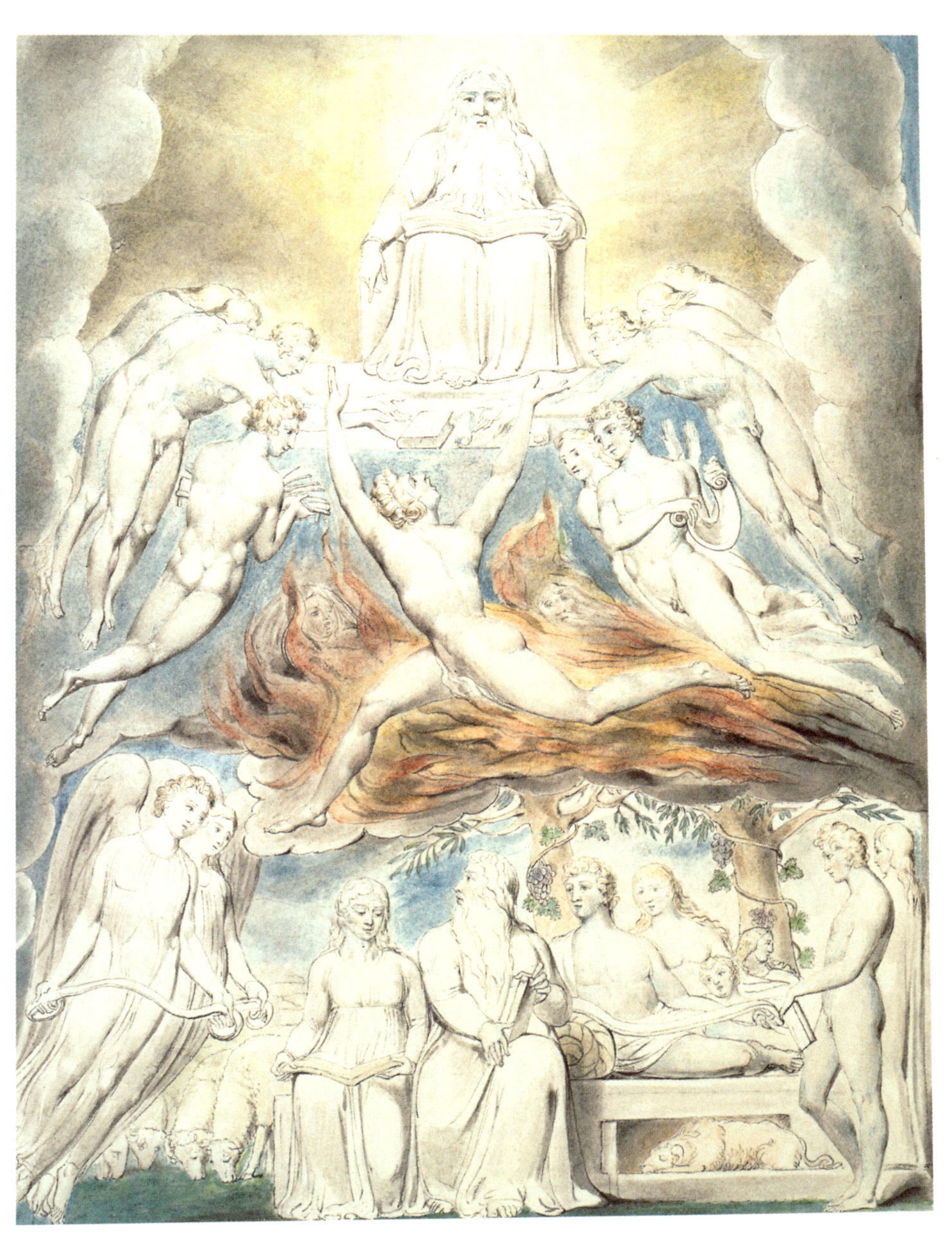

COLOR PLATE II **Satan Before the Throne of God** SEE NO. 2A, PAGE 25

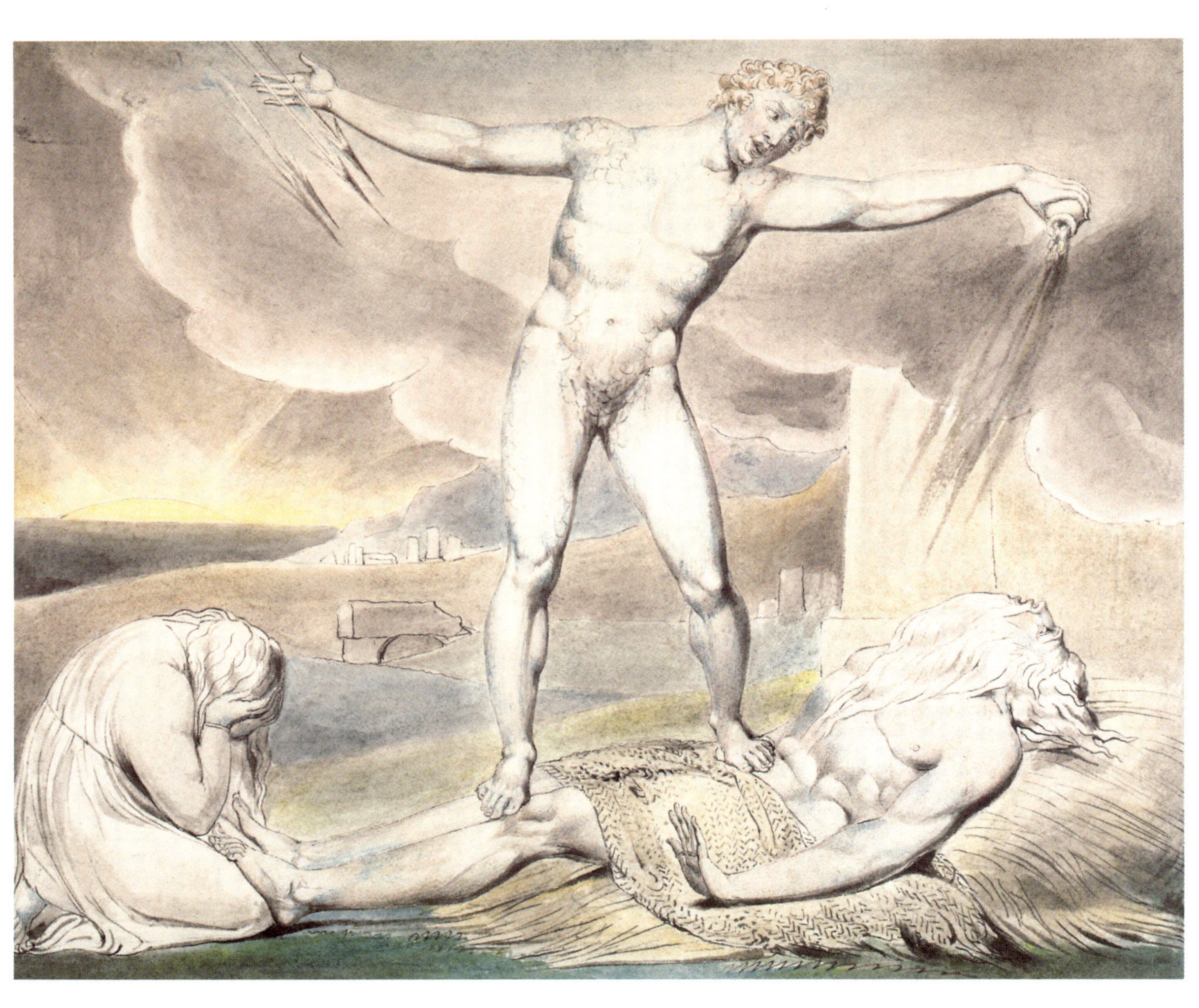

COLOR PLATE III **Satan Smiting Job with Boils** SEE NO. 6A, PAGE 35

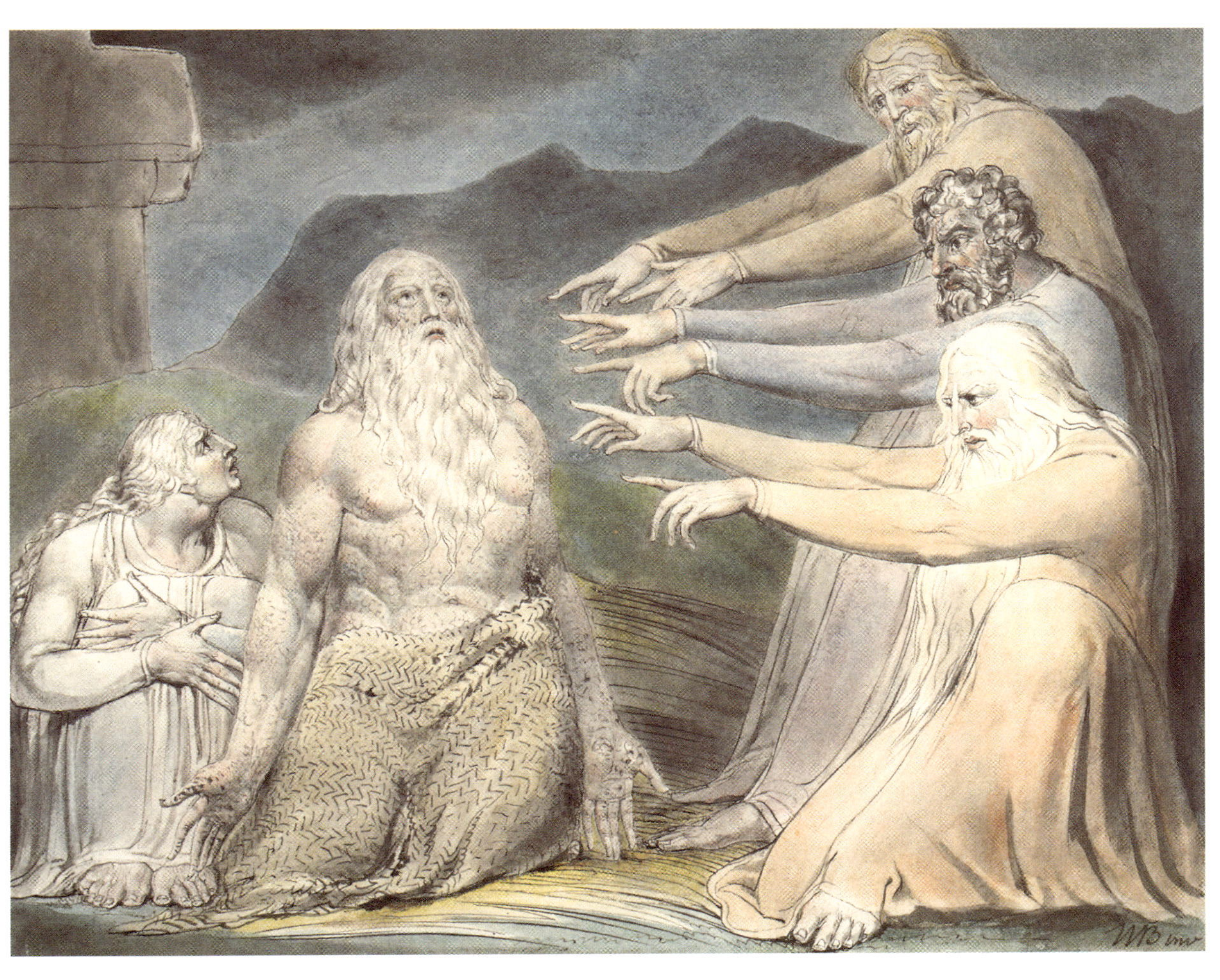

COLOR PLATE IV Job Rebuked by His Friends SEE NO. 10A, PAGE 45

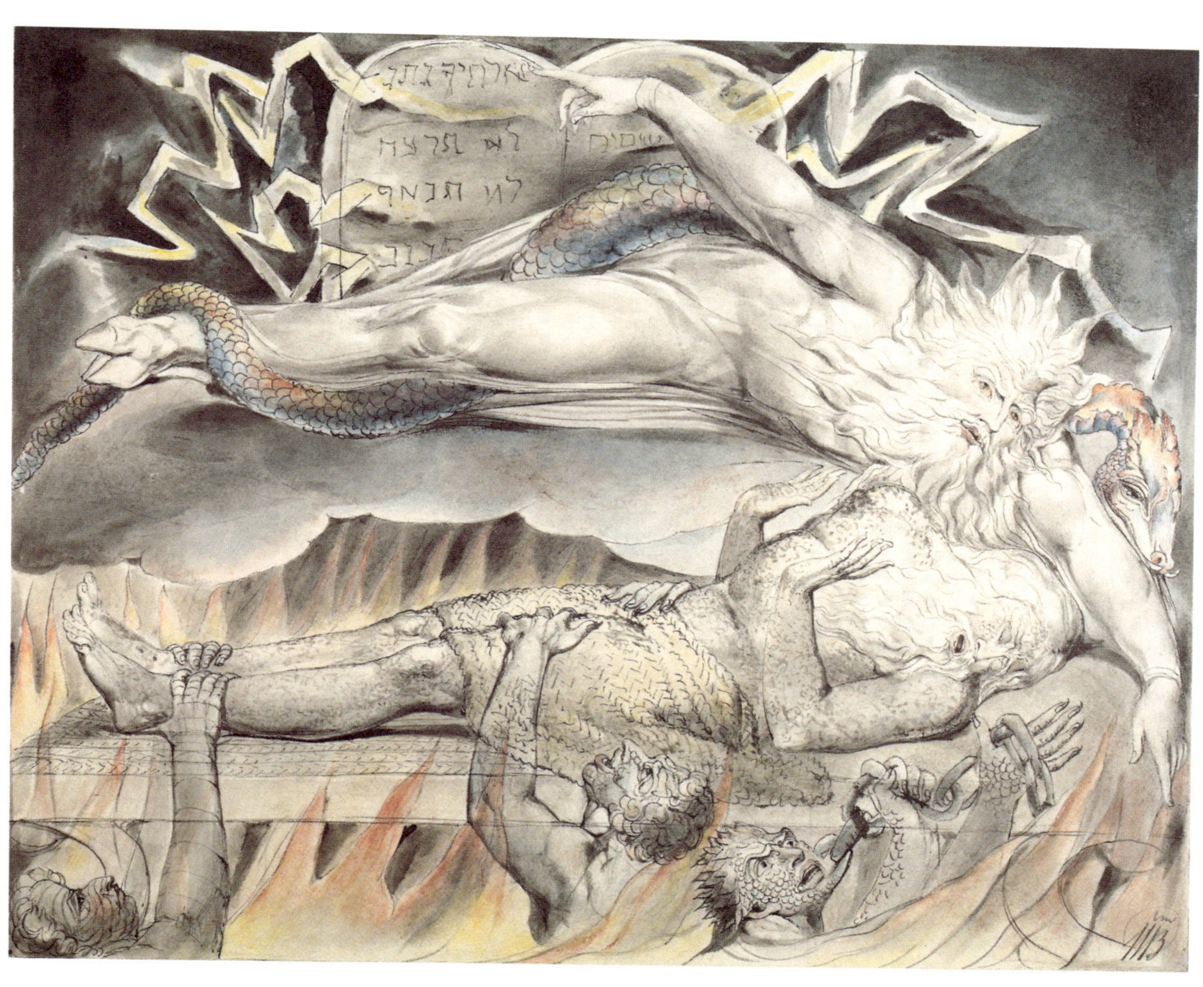

COLOR PLATE V **Job's Evil Dreams** SEE NO. 11A, PAGE 49

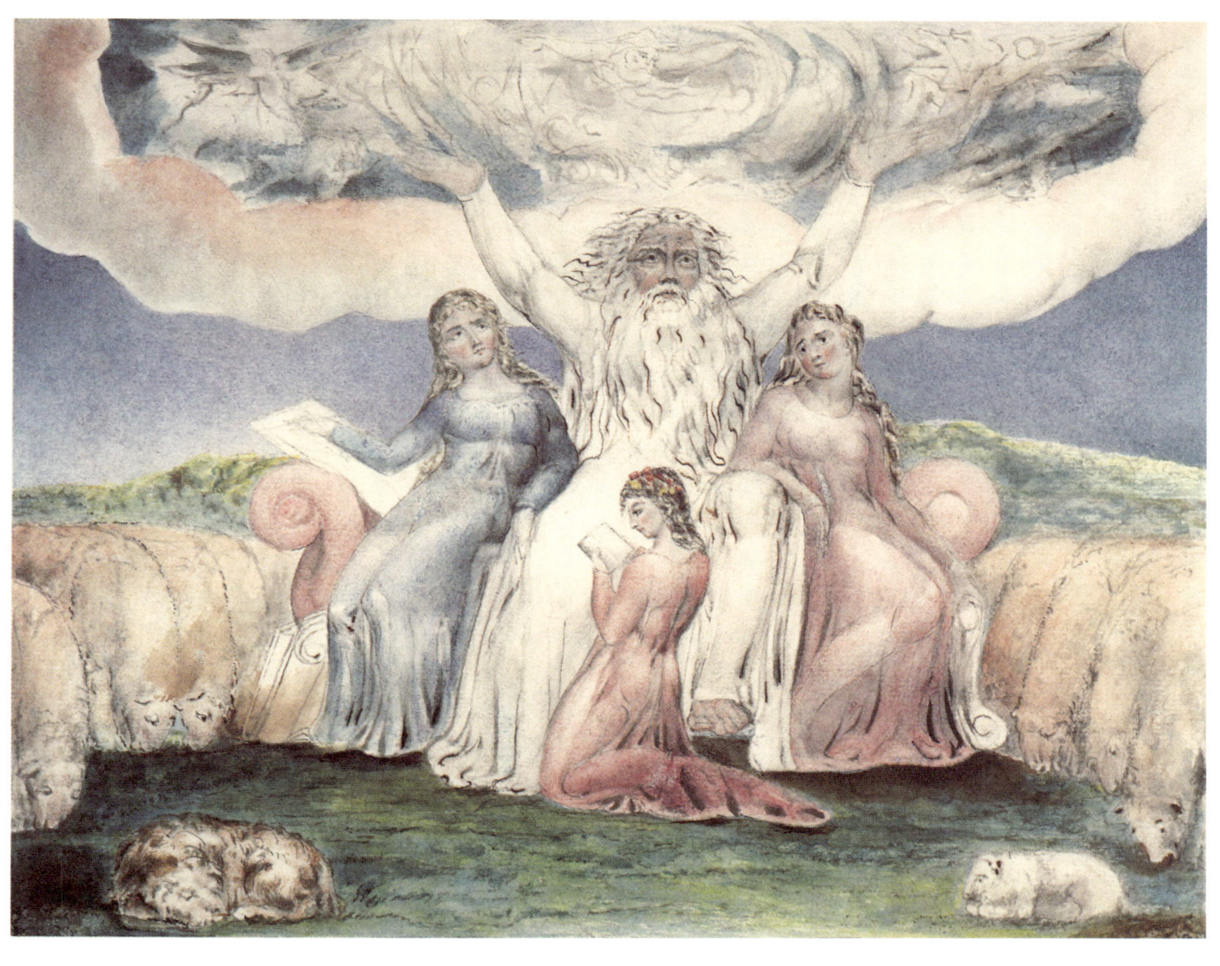

COLOR PLATE VI Job and His Daughters SEE NO. 20A, PAGE 69

Blake's Studies and Engravings for the *Book of Job*

INTRODUCTION

Blake's preoccupation with the story of Job lasted over forty years. A single impression of his untitled engraving of Job[1] can be dated about 1785–6, and there are a number of preliminary drawings from around 1785 that are connected with this engraving.[2] The second state of the line engraving of Job (entitled *Job*) was published in 1793 and inscribed: *Job / What Is Man That Thou Shouldst Try Him Every Moment.*[3]

It was, however, for his most constant patron, Thomas Butts, that Blake produced first a tempera painting, *Job and His Daughters* (Butlin no. 394), in about 1799–1800; then an individual watercolor, *Job Confessing His Presumption to God Who Answers from the Whirlwind* (Butlin no. 461), as part of his large Biblical series for Butts; and finally, in about 1804–7, a series of watercolors devoted entirely to the story of Job (see color plates I–VI). Blake used the early Tate drawing—*Job, His Wife and Friends: The Complaint of Job* (Butlin no. 162)—for both the watercolor and the engraving of *Job Rebuked by His Friends* (see plate 10).

The series of Job watercolors much impressed another of Blake's admirers, John Linnell, who in 1821 produced outlines from these watercolors that Blake added to in ink and watercolor. This set of twenty-one designs for Job are known as the "Linnell set" (Butlin nos. 551.1–21).

Other drawings in pen, ink, and watercolor of single subjects from the *Book of Job* were probably done about this time, e.g. *Job and His Daughters* (Butlin no. 556) and *Job Sacrificing for His Friends* (Butlin no. 552). These drawings probably mark the beginning of Linnell's interest in commissioning the complete series, *Illustrations of the Book of Job.*

Two years later, Blake signed an agreement with Linnell to create engraved illustrations for the *Book of Job*, which he finished in 1826 after making a series of preliminary sketches. Another set of watercolors, now called the "New Zealand set," surfaced in 1928 and are thought to be copies of the engravings.

Included in this catalogue are reproductions of and comments on one of the complete sets of the engravings, which is owned by the Virginia Museum of Fine Arts; six of the twenty-one original watercolors Blake painted in 1804–7 for Thomas Butts (Pierpont Morgan Library); the rapid drawings made in preparation for the engravings commissioned by John Linnell (Fitzwilliam Museum, Cambridge, England); and six watercolors from the New Zealand set (Yale Center for British Art, Paul Mellon Collection). Color plates of the six Butts watercolors precede this section, and they are also reproduced in black and white to accompany the relevant engravings, as are the drawings and New Zealand watercolors.

Connoisseurs of Blake's individual watercolor technique—which was not inconsiderable, with its own beauties of coloring, felicities of line, and sensitivity of touch—can compare the New Zealand watercolors with Blake's other watercolors and the engraved plates. (Watercolors from the Linnell set, now mostly at the Fogg Art Museum, Harvard, could not be borrowed because of the restrictions of the original donor's bequest.) Seeing the various stages of Blake's work on the *Book of Job* also makes it possible to appreciate both the changes he made in his designs and the sheer concentrated labor he expended in the production of the plates.

The Butts Set of Watercolors

Pierpont Morgan Library, New York

The six Butts watercolors reproduced in this book were selected for their dramatic power and their relevance to Blake's interpretation of the *Book of Job. Job and His Daughters* (COLOR PLATE VI, NO. 20A) has been chosen because of its obvious differences to the engraved plate (PLATE 20), being set out-of-doors. Its clear differences of style and handling, however, suggest that it may have been a later addition, perhaps done with the collaboration of Mrs. Blake. It thus provides an interesting problem of connoisseurship in comparison with the other five, and with the six watercolors from the New Zealand set (see page 16).

The provenance of the Butts set is: Thomas Butts; Thomas Butts, Jr.; sold to Richard Monkton Milnes, 1st Lord Houghton; his son, 1st Marquess of Crewe; sold Sotheby's, March 30, 1903; bought by Messrs. Quaritch, from whom purchased by John Pierpont Morgan.

Martin Butlin and David Bindman provide further commentary and references for this series.[4]

The Preliminary Sketches

Fitzwilliam Museum, Cambridge, England

On March 25, 1823, Blake signed a Memorandum of Agreement with John Linnell, which reads as follows:

> W. Blake agrees to Engrave the Set of Plates from his own Designs of Job's Captivity in number twenty, for John Linnell—and John Linnell agrees to pay William Blake five pounds pr. Plate or one hundred pounds for the Set, part before and the remainder when the Plates are finished, as Mr. Blake may require it, besides which J. Linnell agrees to give W. Blake one hundred pounds more out of the Profits of the work as the receipts will admit it (signed) J. Linnell, Willm Blake N.B. J.L. to find Copper Plates.

On the verso of the agreement is a cash receipt dated March 25 for the copper plates, which are not identical in size and may have been bought secondhand.

Blake produced his small-scale sketches for the engravings within the year. These drawings are on fifteen sheets of paper that, as indicated by the stitch marks, were previously bound, so that they originally formed a sketchbook of thirty leaves measuring approximately 8½ by 5¾ inches (222 by 145 mm). Two leaves of printed sheets from Hayley's *Ballads* of 1803, approximately 9¼ by 5¾ inches (235 by 145 mm), served as wrapping. On the first of these sheets, on the side that served as the outermost wrapping, Blake experimented with the monogram *WB*, sometimes adding to it *inv. & sc.* 1823; on the verso of this sheet are a list of the apostles, a sketch for the back of Job's head in plate 18, and two studies of a dog's head. The second sheet bears an inscription by John Linnell: *These are Mr. Blakes reduced drawings & studies for the Engravings of the Book of Job done for me John Linnell.*

The drawings are executed mostly in pencil, with some watercolor. The measurements given in this book are those of the actual design area, not the size of the sheet.

The provenance of the sketches is: John Linnell by descent; sold Christie's March 15, 1918, lot 150; bought Carfax for T.H. Riches; bequeathed to the Fitzwilliam Museum with a life interest to his widow (née Linnell), received 1950.

Martin Butlin and David Bindman provide further commentary and references for these sketches.[5]

The Engraved *Illustrations of the Book of Job*

Virginia Museum of Fine Arts, Richmond

The engravings which Linnell commissioned, and for which he retained the copyright, were produced relatively quickly, considering their complication. Between 1823, when Linnell acquired the copper plates, and early 1825, Blake demonstrated his skill as an engraver by producing both images and lettering for twenty-two plates. By 1826 the sales were well under way. Unlike Blake's other endeavors, however, he seems to have allowed a commercial printer, J. Lahee of Castle St., Oxford Market, London, to print the plates under his supervision. (The plates still exist and are now in the British Museum). The label that was attached to the various editions was printed in a mixture of types by a Mr. Tickman at 10s-6d (that is, half a guinea) for 500 labels. These seem to have been printed on blue paper, but the label on the Virginia Museum's set is much faded.

Blake's prices started at £3-3-0 (3 guineas; £2-12s-6d for booksellers), for an edition of 100 plain copies, which, being the cheapest, were sold out by 1863. Proof copies were £5-5-0 (five guineas), although the label is inscribed £6-6-0, of which 215 were printed. Noblemen were charged more: for example, the Earl of Egremont paid £6-6-0 (six guineas), while a copy acquired by the Royal Librarian for King George IV cost £10-10-0 (10 guineas). A further edition from the original plates was published in 1874 on India paper. According to Butlin, there were in fact no profits, but Linnell gave Blake an additional £50 on top of about £1 a week. Blake received £54 in 1823, £46.7.9 in 1824, and £49.6.6 in 1825. On July 14, 1826, he signed a receipt for £150 for the copyright and twenty-two plates, including one for the title page.

The veracity of the edition in the collection of the Virginia Museum of Fine Arts is without question. Plates 2, 4, and 10 are watermarked *J WHATMAN 1825*, and plate 15 is watermarked *J WHATMAN TURKEY MILL 1825*. Although Barbara Bryant has assiduously traced the various printed editions, through Linnell's accounts, the provenance of the Virginia Museum's edition is not clear.[6] The label bears an elaborate monogram that may be read as "JS." The only "JS" who appears in the history of early sales of the printed edition is Joseph Strutt, Jr., who bought Sir Thomas Lawrence's copy at his sale in 1830, but this identification is only conjecture. The edition was purchased for the Virginia Museum of Fine Arts in 1973 from Erik Ewertz, Baltimore, Maryland, through The Arthur and Margaret Glasgow Fund.

Linnell was an energetic salesman for the artist he so admired, and his accounts and letters reveal how hard he pushed. But at the end of the nineteenth century there were still proof copies to be had. The few individual plates that are hand-colored, perhaps by Blake or his wife, Catherine, are extremely rare, but the Virginia Museum copy indicates the extent to which Blake and Linnell strived to produce the best possible examples of Blake's work; apart from some foxing due to the interleaved wrappers, the prints are in excellent condition, revealing all the richness of Blake's printmaking technique.

The sizes of the actual inner images within the decorated borders vary from 3 5/8 by 4 5/8 inches to 5 3/8 by 4 inches. Blake's plates were approximately 6 5/8 by 8 1/4 inches, though the plate marks are not entirely identical. Nearly all of Blake's inscriptions are taken from the Authorized (King James) Version of the Bible, which he often amended by changing the order of the works and verses.

For bibliographical references see David Bindman's *Blake's Illustrations of the Book of Job*, particularly Robert Essick's essay, which gives a detailed account of Blake's engraving techniques and a description of the proof copies. Barbara Bryant's essay reveals in great detail the sales of individual copies as recorded in Linnell's accounts.[7] Equally detailed, with a comparison of related drawings to the engraved plates, an interpretation of the iconography, and references to previous descriptions and related scenes in the history of art, is Bo Lindberg's *William Blake's Illustrations to the Book of Job.*[8]

The New Zealand Set of Pencil and Watercolor Illustrations

Yale Center for British Art, New Haven

The existence of the New Zealand set of twenty-two pen and ink illustrations of the *Book of Job* was unknown until 1928, when it was sold by the daughters of Albin Martin (1813–1888), a student of John Linnell, Blake's associate. The records of John Linnell reveal neither the acquisition nor disposal of the set, leaving the question of Blake's authorship of the set in doubt.

The question of authenticity must therefore be settled on stylistic grounds. Laurence Binyon, Geoffrey Keynes, and others accepted the set as genuine, wholly or in part, because the drawings occasionally vary from the engravings and follow earlier designs. Anthony Blunt argued that if a work of art combines details from two demonstrably authentic works but contains no independent traits (or only insignificant ones) there is a strong suggestion that the work is a copy. Bo Lindberg, David Bindman, and Martin Butlin agreed with Blunt's reasoning, and Butlin excluded the entire set from his 1981 catalogue raisonné of Blake's work.[9] It should be noted that the size of these designs, drawn to the exact edge, may also denote that they are small copies, although of course they may have been subsequently trimmed.

The New Zealand set may in fact be a copy by Linnell and his circle, including Mrs. Linnell, or by Albin Martin from the Linnell set and the published engravings. The six images from the New Zealand set (Yale Center for British Art) are included in this exhibition for purposes of comparison with the authentic watercolors from the Butts set and the engravings (see plates 1, 2, 6, 10, 14, and 20). They are in watercolor with pen and black ink. Their provenance is: probably John Linnell; his pupil Albin Martin (b. 1813); his daughters, Miss Fanny Martin and Mrs. E. J. Hickson; sold Sotheby's, London, December 17–21, 1928, lot 139; bought Gabriel Wells (1862–1946); Philip Hofer (1898–1984), by 1933–1941; from whom purchased through Thomas J. Gannon by Paul Mellon, 1941, who gave them to Yale Center for British Art in 1992. For bibliographical references, see Martin Butlin, David Bindman, and Patrick Noon.[10]

RIGHT: **Original cover for Blake's *Illustrations of the Book of Job.***
Virginia Museum of Fine Arts Purchase,
The Arthur and Margaret Glasgow Fund, 73.80.1/22

Notes

1. Previously in the Keynes collection; see Bindman 1978, no. 6.
2. Butlin 1981, nos. 162–64. Hereafter "Butlin no." refers to the Butlin catalogue numbers.
3. Bindman 1978, no. 144.
4. Butlin 1981, pp. 410 ff., nos. 550–59, pl. 697–717; Bindman 1987a.
5. Butlin 1981, pp. 425 ff., no. 557, pl. 758–86; Bindman 1970, pp. 45 ff., no. 39 [1–29]; Bindman 1987a.
6. Bindman 1987a, pp. 103-44.
7. Ibid., pp. 35-102; 103–44.
8. Lindberg 1973, pp. 183–352.
9. See Butlin 1981, pp. 409–10, for references and discussion of this question.
10. Butlin 1981, pp. 409–10; Bindman 1987b, 1:11-27; Noon 1997, pp. 3–4; 85–86.

ILLUSTRATIONS

OF THE

Book of Job,

IN TWENTY-ONE PLATES, INVENTED AND ENGRAVED BY

WILLIAM BLAKE,

Author of Designs to "Blair's Grave," "Young's Night Thoughts," &c.

London:

PUBLISHED BY THE AUTHOR, 3, FOUNTAIN COURT, STRAND, AND MR. J. LINNELL, 6, CIRENCESTER PLACE, FITZROY SQUARE.

MARCH, 1826.

95

Prints £ 3 . 3 . ***Proofs £*** 6 6

Title Page to the Illustrations

ENGRAVING; DESIGN AREA 7 3/8 X 5 3/4 INCHES (189 X 145 MM)

INSCRIBED IN HEBREW, *The Book of Job;* IN GOTHIC LETTERS, *ILLUSTRATIONS of / THE BOOK / of JOB;* IN ROMAN LETTERS, *Invented & Engraved / by William Blake /* 1825; AND ON THE LOWER MARGIN, *London Published as the Act directs March 8: 1825 by William Blake* NO. *3 Fountain Court Strand.*

The small sketches in the Fitzwilliam Museum do not contain a draft for the title page, for which there is a pencil sketch in the National Gallery of Art, Washington (Rosenwald Collection), showing that the design was a later addition (Butlin 1981, no. 538).

Around the lower part of the title page, which is resting on a cloud, are seven angels, sometimes interpreted as showing the path of experience. They may also be recording the acts of humanity.

Virginia Museum of Fine Arts Purchase, The Arthur and Margaret Glasgow Fund, 73.80.1/22

REFERENCE: Bindman 1987, pp. 57 (text); see also Title Page.

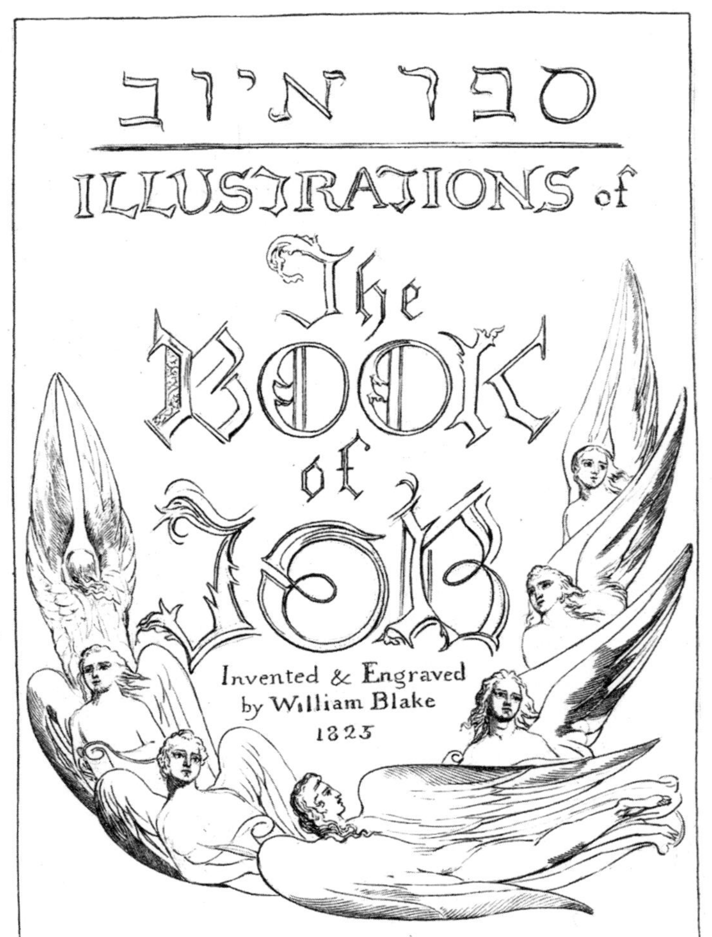

London Published as the Act directs March 8:1825 by William Blake No 3 Fountain Court Strand

Our Father which art in Heaven hallowed be thy Name

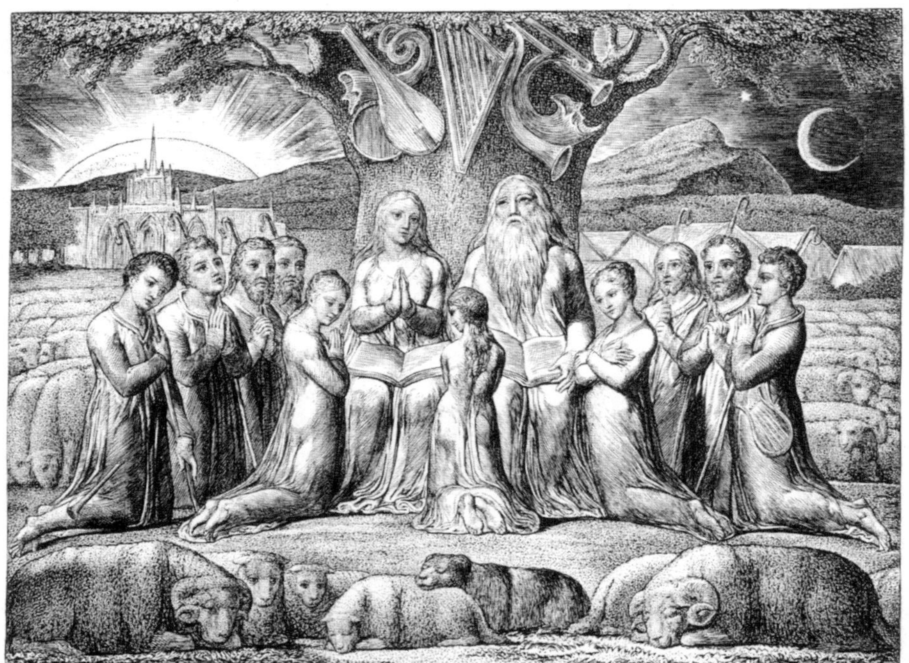

Thus did Job continually

There was a Man in the Land of Uz whose Name was Job. & that Man was perfect & upright

The Letter Killeth
The Spirit giveth Life

It is Spiritually Discerned

& one that feared God & eschewed Evil. & there was born unto him Seven Sons & Three Daughters

W Blake inv & sculp

London. Published as the Act directs. March 8: 1828. by Willm Blake No 3 Fountain Court Strand.

PLATE 1

Job and His Family: Thus Did Job Continually

ENGRAVING; DESIGN 7 1/8 X 5 11/16 INCHES (181 X 150 MM)

INSCRIBED ABOVE THE IMAGE: *Our Father which art in Heaven / hallowed be thy Name* (MATTHEW 6:9); BELOW THE IMAGE: *Thus did Job continually* (JOB 1:5), FOLLOWED BY, AT BOTTOM LEFT, *There was a Man in the / Land of Uz whose Name / was Job. & that Man / was perfect & upright,* AND, AT BOTTOM RIGHT, *& one that feared God / & eschewed Evil & there / was born unto him Seven / Sons & Three Daughters* (JOB 1:1-2). ON AN ALTAR IN THE MIDDLE OF THIS QUOTATION IS *The Letter Killeth / The Spirit giveth Life / It is Spiritually Discerned* (2 CORINTHIANS 3:6 AND 1 CORINTHIANS 2:14). SIGNED ON PLATE *WBlake inv & sculp.* THE PUBLISHER'S IMPRINT UNDERNEATH HAS THE WRONG DATE OF 1828.

In the original Butts watercolor (NO. 1A), part of the Lord's Prayer is inscribed on the setting sun. There are four connected drawings in the Fitzwilliam sketchbook (NOS. 1B–D).

Although the Gothic church in the background and the inscription of the Lord's Prayer imply that Job is a Christian (the Swedenborgians believed that Job was one of the Christian priests in the Old Testament), the musical instruments hanging unused in the tree suggest that Job has allowed the rituals and law of the Church to stifle the workings of the imagination and the spirit in his own life and that of his family.

The bottom margin has the heads of a bull on the left and a ram on the right, which stood for Moses and Christ (see also plate 21).

Virginia Museum of Fine Arts Purchase, The Arthur and Margaret Glasgow Fund, 73.80.2/22

REFERENCE: Bindman 1987a, pp. 57–60 (text); pl. 1.

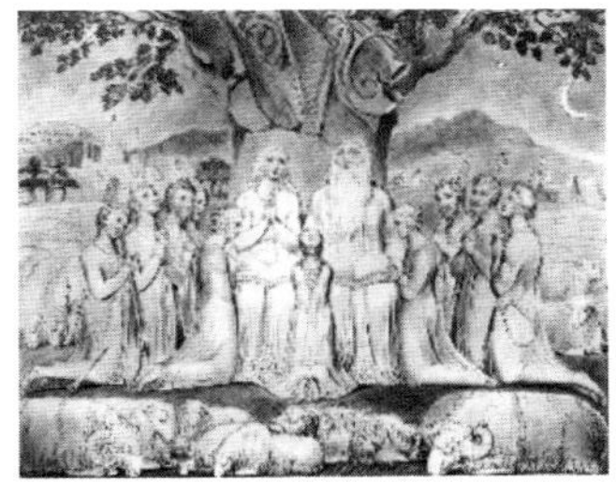

1A **JOB AND HIS FAMILY** CA. 1804–7
(COLOR PLATE I)
PEN AND WATERCOLOR
8 7/8 X 10 13/18 INCHES (225 X 274 MM)
INSCRIBED AT LEFT, CUT SHORT BY HORIZON: *Our Father which art in Heavn Hallowed be thy Name thy will be. . . .*

The Pierpont Morgan Library, New York, III, 45, PLATE 1

REFERENCE: Butlin 1981, p. 411, no. 550.1, pl. 697

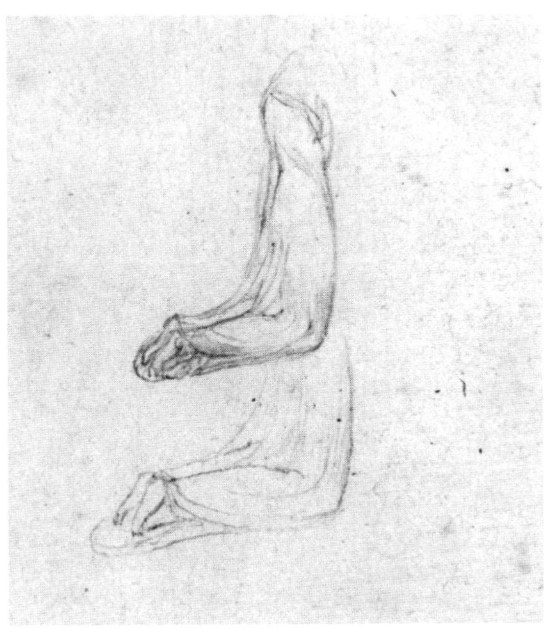

1B **TWO STUDIES FOR JOB AND HIS FAMILY** CA. 1823
PENCIL
APPROXIMATELY 3 1/8 X 1 3/4 INCHES (79 X 45 MM)

Two studies for the left-hand kneeling daughter in plate 1.

The Syndics of the Fitzwilliam Museum, Cambridge, England, PD.48A-1950

REFERENCE: Bindman 1970, p. 47, no. 39(1)

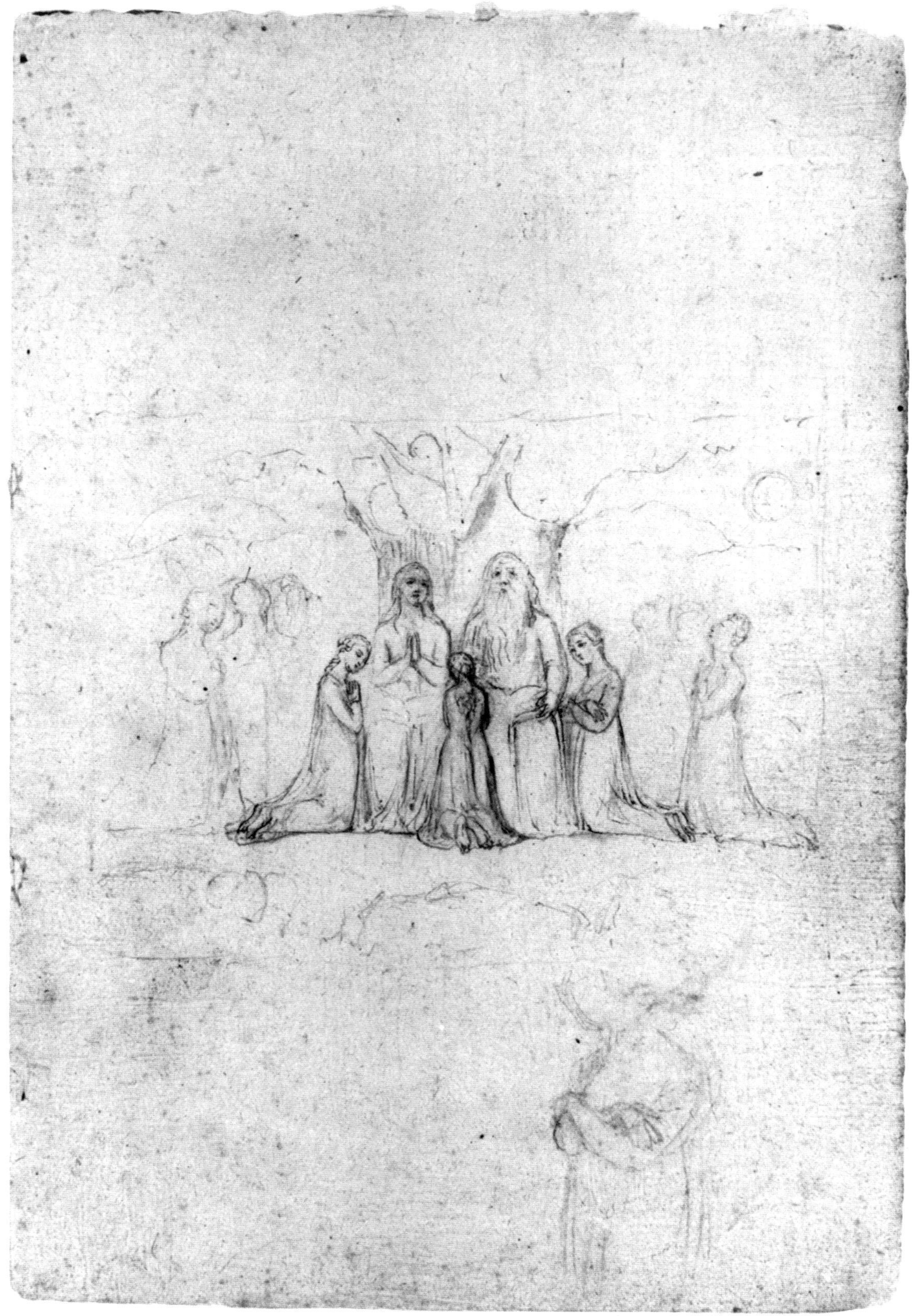

1C Job and His Family [LEFT] CA. 1823
PEN, PENCIL, AND WHITE HEIGHTENING
MAIN DESIGN 2 7/8 X 4 3/4 INCHES
(73 X 120 MM)

The main design is a study for the whole composition; below is a larger study for the daughter to the right of the central group. There is no inscription in the sun as in the Butts watercolor.

The Syndics of the Fitzwilliam Museum, Cambridge, England, PD.27–1950

REFERENCE: Bindman 1970, p. 47, no. 39(2)

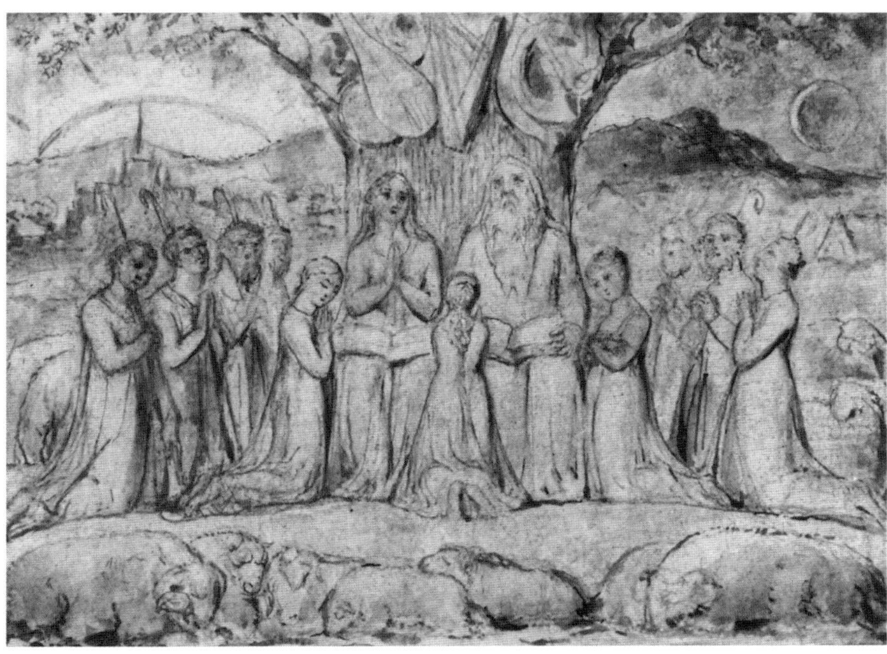

1D Job and His Family [ABOVE] CA. 1823
PENCIL, WATERCOLOR, AND WHITE HEIGHTENING
MAIN DESIGN 3 5/8 X 4 3/4 INCHES (92 X 120 MM)

INSCRIBED *1*, top right

This is closer to the engraving. There are indications of Blake's designs for the margin.

The Syndics of the Fitzwilliam Museum, Cambridge, England, PD.26–1950

REFERENCE: Bindman 1970, p. 47, no. 39(3)

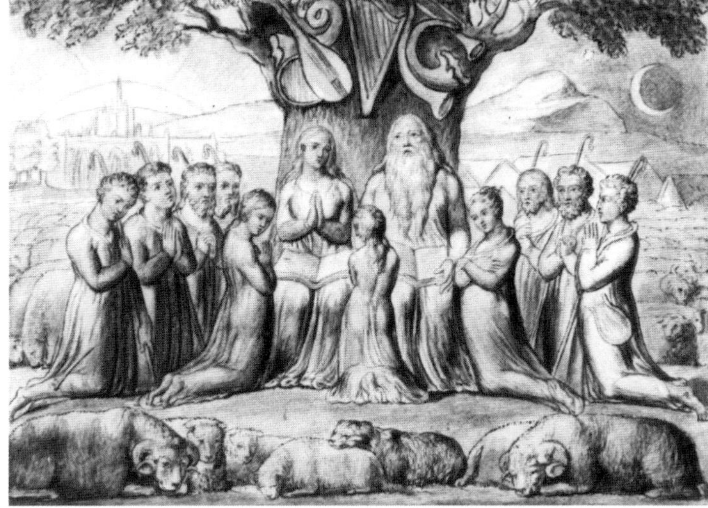

1E Job and His Family [RIGHT] CA. 1826
WATERCOLOR, PEN, AND BLACK INK
3 1/2 X 4 5/8 INCHES (90 X 117 MM)

Yale Center for British Art, New Haven, Paul Mellon Collection, B.1992.8.7(2)

REFERENCE: Bindman 1987a, pl. 1c; 1:12; 2:pl.1

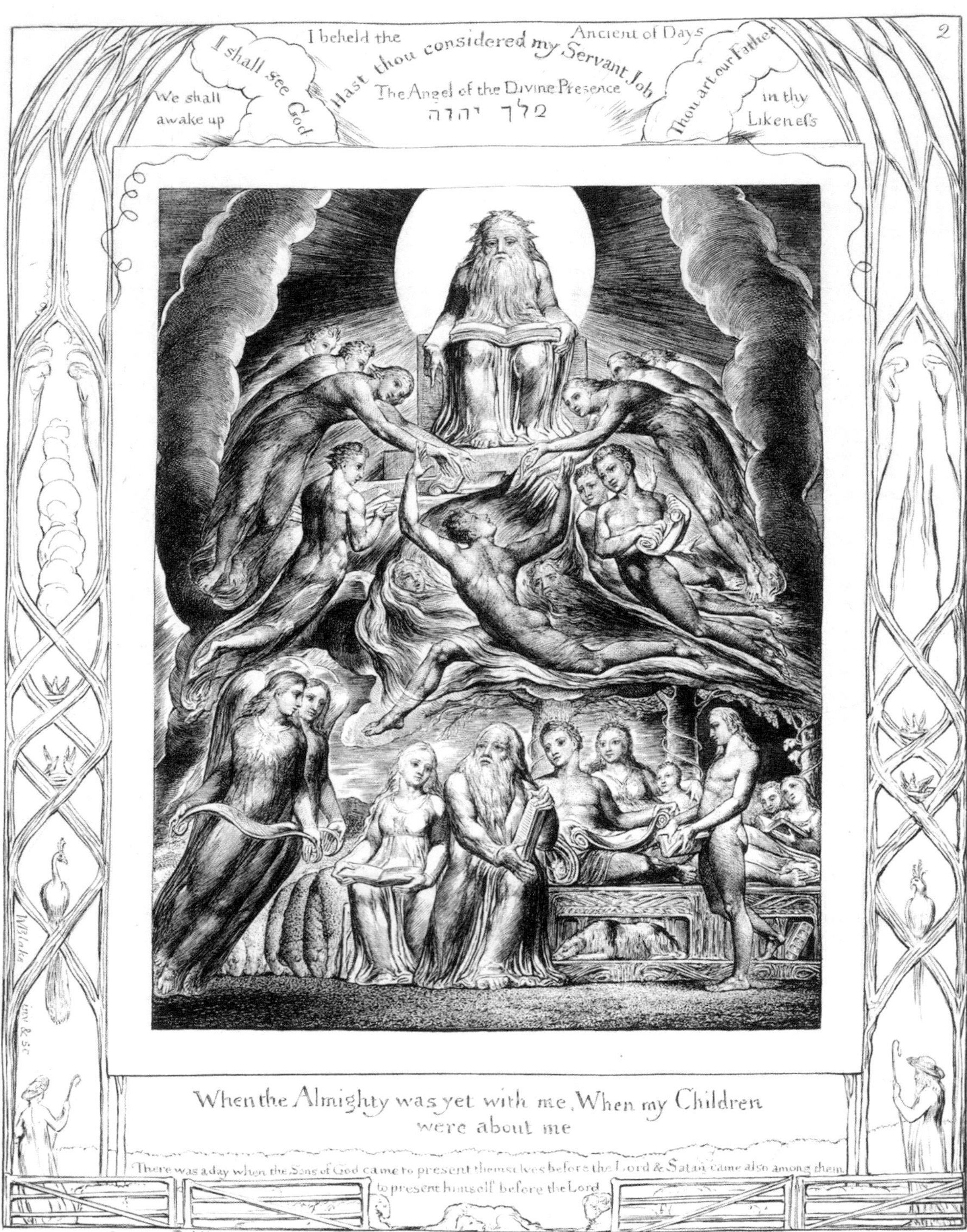

London Published as the Act directs March 8: 1825 by Will.m Blake N.3 Fountain Court Strand

PLATE 2

Satan Before the Throne of God

ENGRAVING; DESIGN 7 3/8 X 5 7/8 INCHES (200 X 149 MM)

INSCRIBED IN THE MIDDLE SECTION OF THE TOP BORDER, IN DESCENDING ORDER: *I beheld the / Ancient of Days* (DANIEL 7:9); *Hast thou considered my Servant Job* (JOB 1:8); *The Angel of the Divine Presence* (ISAIAH 63:9); AND, IN SIMPLIFIED HEBREW, *King Jehovah.* THE VERSE *We shall / awake up / in thy / Likeness* (PSALMS 17:5) IS DIVIDED AND PLACED TO THE FAR LEFT AND RIGHT OF THE TOP BORDER, NEXT TO CLOUDS THAT CONTAIN *I shall see God* (JOB 19:26) AND *Thou art our Father* (ISAIAH 64:8). INSCRIBED BELOW THE IMAGE: *When the Almighty was yet with me. When my Children / were about me* (JOB 29:5) AND *There was a day when the Sons of God came to present themselves before the Lord & Satan came also among them / to present himself before the Lord* (JOB 1:6). SIGNED ON PLATE IN LEFT MARGIN: *WBlake inv. & sc., with publisher's imprint underneath.* WATERMARK: *J Whatman 1825.*

Gothic trelliswork, incorporating nesting birds, a peacock, a pheasant, and praying figures, surrounds the image. At the bottom, on the right and left, a shepherd and shepherdess (perhaps Job and his wife), tend a fold of sheep with the help of the sheep dog resting in the center.

From His throne in the upper part of the image God points earthward toward Job as Satan challenges him from below: in response to God's question, "Hast thou considered my servant Job," Satan answers that Job "will curse thee to thy face" if his possessions are threatened. In the end, God gives Satan leave to try him. Beneath, Job, with his family around him, holds the scriptures in his hand and appears to inquire of the angels what he has done wrong.

Virginia Museum of Fine Arts Purchase, The Arthur and Margaret Glasgow Fund, 73.80.3/22

REFERENCE: Bindman 1987, pp. 60–62 (text); pl. 2

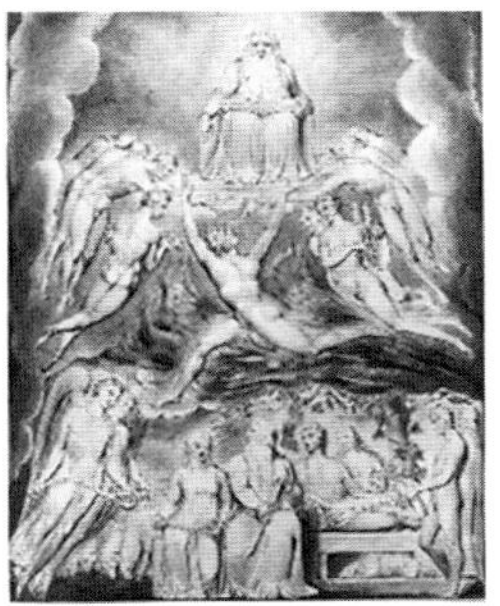

2A SATAN BEFORE THE THRONE OF GOD
(COLOR PLATE II) CA. 1804–7
PEN AND WATERCOLOR
11 11/16 X 8 15/16 INCHES (296 X 228 MM)

The Pierpont Morgan Library,
New York, III, 45, PLATE 2

REFERENCE: Butlin 1981, p. 411, no. 550.2, pl. 698

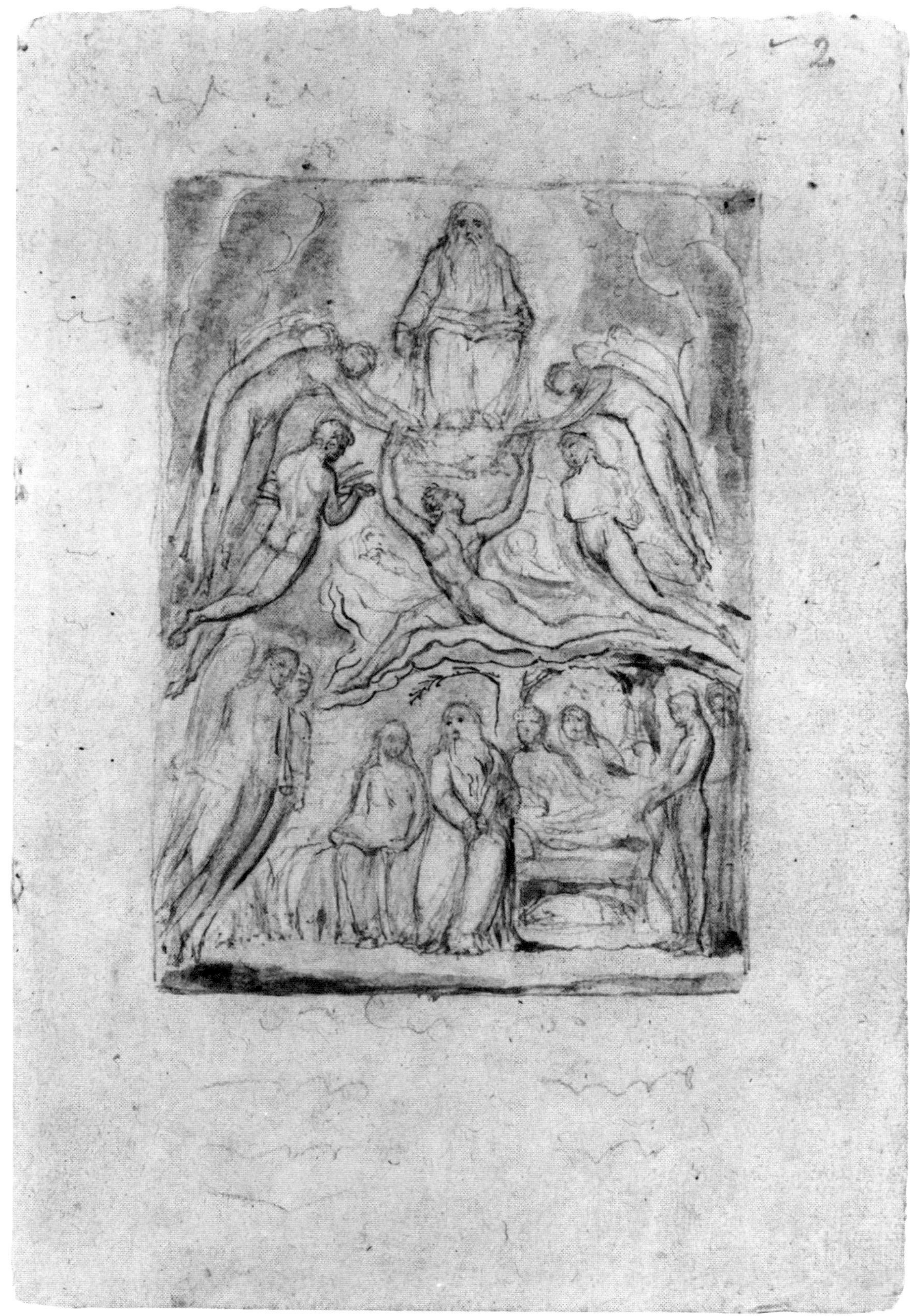

2B Satan Before the Throne of God CA. 1823
PENCIL, PEN, INDIA INK, BLUE AND GREY WASH
5 7/16 X 3 13/16 INCHES (139 X 98 MM)

INSCRIBED 2, top right

In the engraving the figures at the right have been slightly altered.

The Syndics of the Fitzwilliam Museum, Cambridge, England, PD.28-1950

REFERENCE: Bindman 1970, p. 47, no. 39(4)

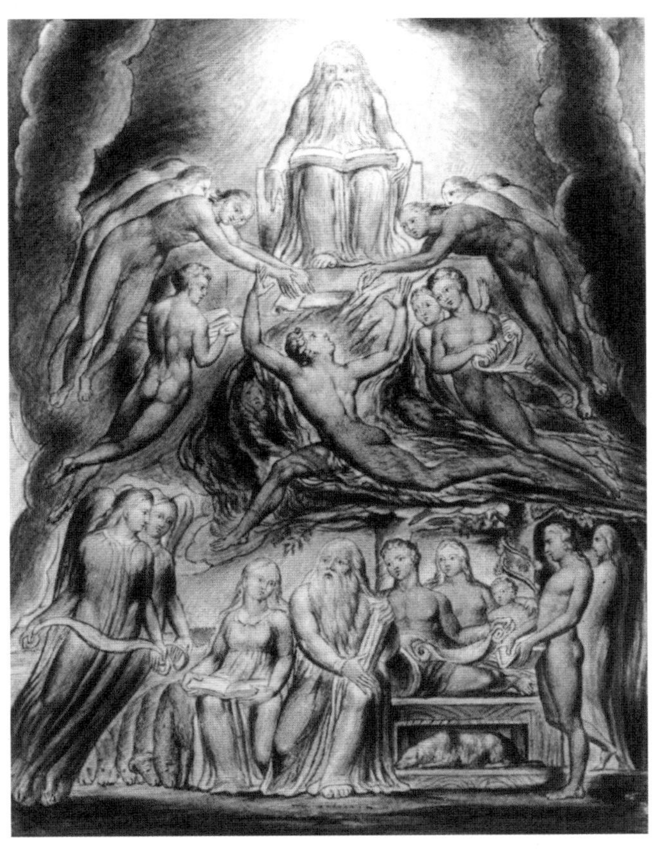

2C Satan Before the Throne of God CA. 1826
PENCIL AND WATERCOLOR
5 1/2 X 4 1/8 INCHES (140 X 105 MM)

Yale Center for British Art, New Haven, Paul Mellon Collection, B.1992.8.7(3)

REFERENCE: Bindman 1987a, pl. 2C; 1987b, 1:12–13; 2:pl. 2

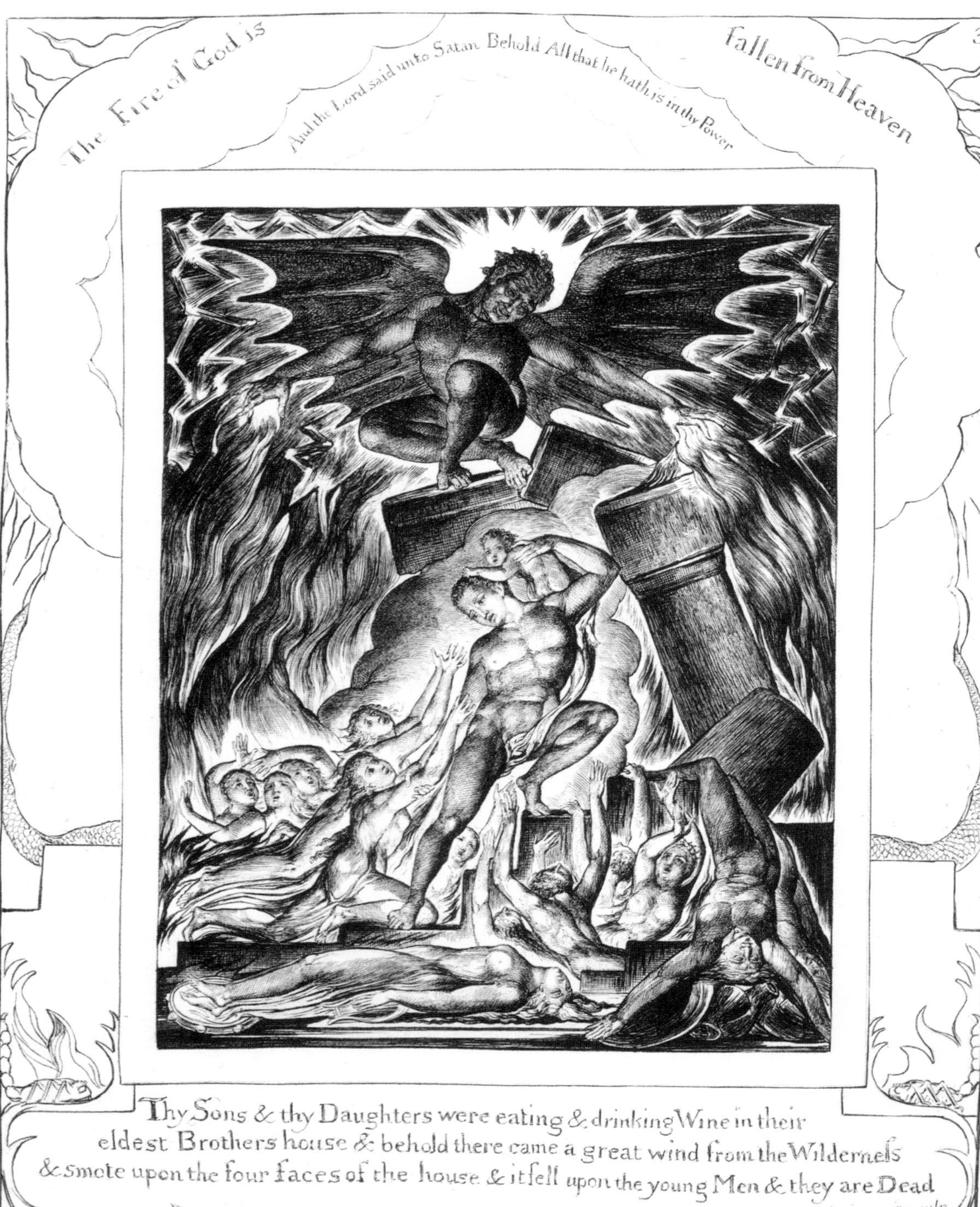

London, Published as the Act directs March 8: 1825 by Will.m Blake No 3 Fountain Court Strand

PLATE 3

Job's Sons and Daughters Overwhelmed by Satan

ENGRAVING; DESIGN 7 3/4 X 5 7/8 INCHES (196 X 150 MM)

INSCRIBED ABOVE THE IMAGE: *The Fire of God is / fallen from Heaven* (JOB 1:16) / *And the Lord said unto Satan Behold All that he hath is in thy Power* (JOB 1:12); BELOW THE IMAGE: *Thy Sons & thy Daughters were eating & drinking Wine in their / eldest Brothers house & behold there came a great wind from the Wilderness / & smote upon the four faces of the house & it fell upon the young Men & they are Dead* (JOB 1:18-19). SIGNED ON PLATE, LOWER RIGHT, WITH PUBLISHER'S IMPRINT UNDERNEATH.

The sons and daughters were eating and drinking in the eldest son's house, which Satan is destroying by fire (rather than by wind as in the biblical text). The figure on the lower right, who is crucified upside down on plates and cups, seems to suggest that hedonistic delights in food and drink make Satan our master, for he easily overpowers those who pursue such worldly pleasures.

In the margins are continued part of the collapsing house, fire, smoke, two scorpions, and a scaly serpent. Satan in the main image now has batlike wings and dominates the scene of disaster.

Virginia Museum of Fine Arts Purchase, The Arthur and Margaret Glasgow Fund, 73.80.4/22

REFERENCE: Bindman 1987a, pp. 63–64 (text); pl. 3

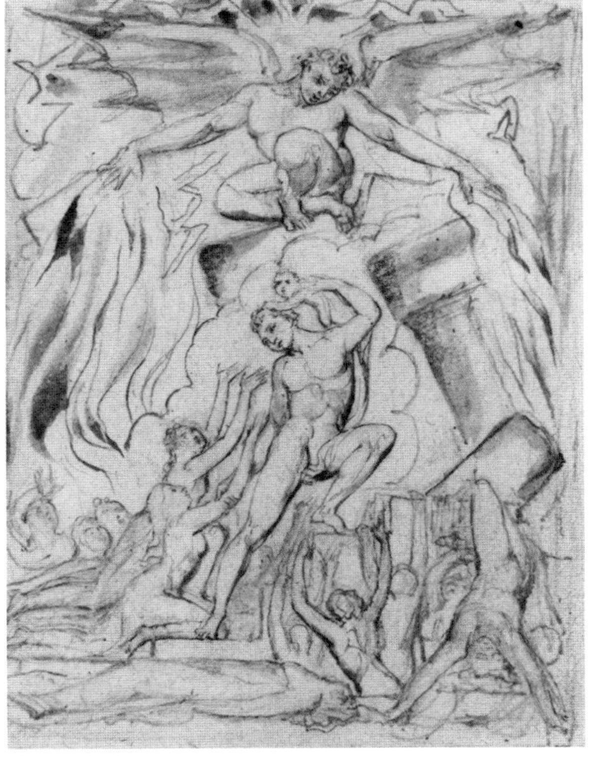

3A JOB'S SONS AND DAUGHTERS OVERWHELMED BY SATAN
CA. 1823
PENCIL, PEN, INDIA INK, AND GREY WASH
5 X 3 3/4 INCHES (127 X 95 MM)

INSCRIBED 3, top right

The Syndics of the Fitzwilliam Museum, Cambridge, England, PD.29-1950

REFERENCE: Bindman 1970, p. 47, no. 39(5)

And there came a Messenger unto Job & said The Oxen were plowing & the Sabeans came down & they have slain the Young Men with the Sword

Going to & fro in the Earth & walking up & down in it

And I only am escaped alone to tell thee.

While he was yet speaking
there came also another & said
The fire of God is fallen from heaven & hath burned up the flocks & the
Young Men & consumed them & I only am escaped alone to tell thee

W Blake invent & sculp

London. Published as the Act directs March 8: 1825 by Willm Blake N° 3 Fountain Court Strand

PLATE 4

The Messengers Tell Job of His Misfortunes

ENGRAVING; DESIGN 7 5/8 X 5 3/4 INCHES (194 X 147 MM)

INSCRIBED ABOVE THE IMAGE: *And there came a Messenger unto Job & said The Oxen were plowing & the Sabeans came down. & they have slain the Young Men with the Sword* (JOB 1:14-15); ON EITHER SIDE OF AN IMAGE OF SATAN ON THE TOP OF THE GLOBE, *Going to & fro in the Earth* AND *& walking up & down in it* (SATAN'S ANSWER TO GOD'S QUESTION, *"Whence comest thou,"* Job 1:7). BELOW THE IMAGE: *And I only am escaped alone to tell thee* (CONTINUATION OF JOB 1:15), AND *While he was yet speaking / there came also another & said / The fire of God is fallen from heaven & hath burned up the flocks & the / Young Men & consumed them & I only am escaped alone to tell thee* (JOB 1:16). SIGNED ON PLATE, LOWER RIGHT, WITH PUBLISHER'S IMPRINT UNDERNEATH. WATERMARK: *J WHATMAN 1825.*

Although the news the messengers bring is disastrous (symbolized by the collapsed figures draped over the upper corners of the borders), Job remains steadfast in his faith, reinforced by the images of the Gothic church at the left, behind the distant messenger (one is still running up the hill), the sturdy (olive?) tree, and the unshakable pillars of his house. For the moment, Satan has been stalled.

The large figure of the running messenger has been taken from the running angel in Raphael's fresco of *Heliodorus Expelled from the Temple,* another example of Blake's tendency to adopt poses from engravings after artists he particularly admired.

Virginia Museum of Fine Arts Purchase, The Arthur and Margaret Glasgow Fund, 73.80.5/22

REFERENCE: Bindman 1987a, pp. 64–66 (text); pl. 4

4A THE MESSENGERS TELL JOB OF HIS MISFORTUNES
CA. 1823
PENCIL, PEN, AND WATERCOLOR
3 5/16 X 4 5/8 INCHES (84 X 117 MM)
INSCRIBED *4*, top right
The Syndics of the Fitzwilliam Museum, Cambridge, England, PD.30-1950
REFERENCE: Bindman 1970, p. 47, no. 39(6)

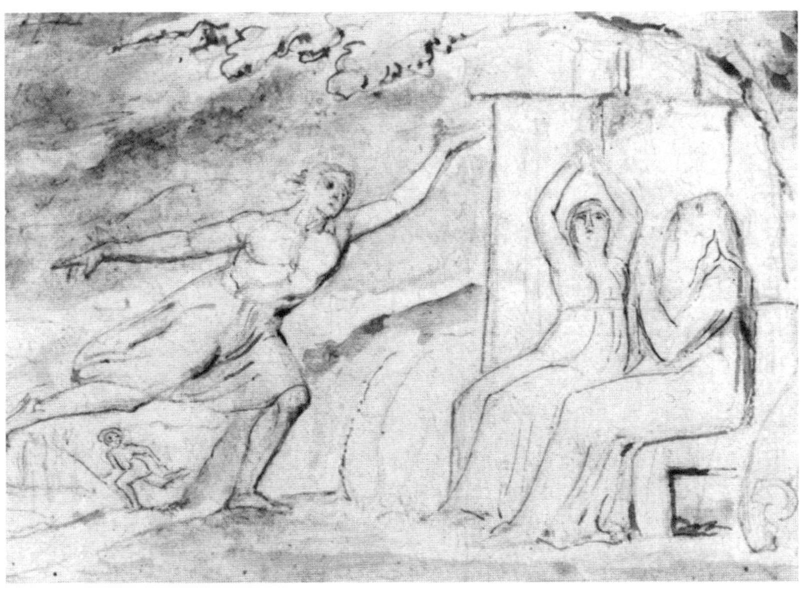

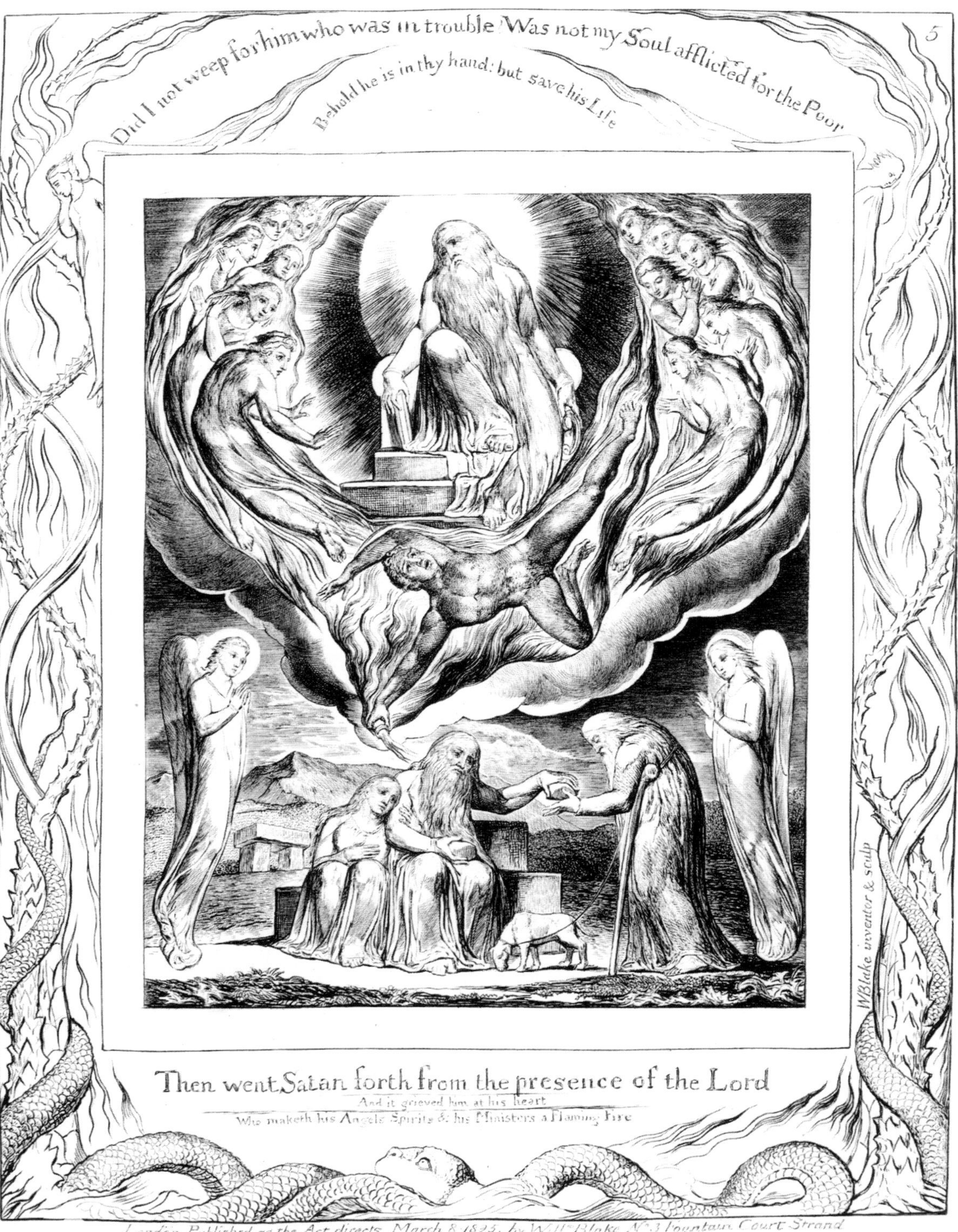
5
Did I not weep for him who was in trouble Was not my Soul afflicted for the Poor
Behold he is in thy hand: but save his Life
Then went Satan forth from the presence of the Lord
And it grieved him at his heart
Who maketh his Angels Spirits & his Ministers a Flaming Fire
WBlake inventor & sculp
London. Published as the Act directs March 8 1825. by Willm Blake N° 3 Fountain Court Strand

PLATE 5

Satan Going Forth from the Presence of God

ENGRAVING; DESIGN 7 5/8 X 5 7/8 INCHES (194 X 149 MM)

INSCRIBED ABOVE THE IMAGE: *Did I not weep for him who was in trouble. Was not my Soul afflicted for the Poor* (JOB 30:25, JOB'S LATER COMPLAINT AGAINST GOD) AND *Behold he is in thy hand: but save his Life* (JOB 2:6, GOD'S COMMAND TO SATAN); BELOW THE IMAGE: *Then went Satan forth from the presence of the Lord* (JOB 2:7); *And it grieved him at his heart* (GENESIS 6:6, GOD'S DISPLEASURE WITH MANKIND); AND *Who maketh his Angel Spirits & his Ministers a Flaming Fire* (PSALM 104:4, PRAISE OF GOD). SIGNED ON PLATE IN RIGHT-HAND MARGIN, WITH PUBLISHER'S IMPRINT UNDERNEATH.

In the top half of the image God almost seems to have abdicated his power to Satan, who is already hurtling toward Job with his poison. Beneath, an impoverished Job gives half a loaf to an elderly beggar, watched over by angels. In the background a circle of stones (a Druid cromlech) perhaps identifies Job as a Druid inhabitant of ancient Britain. The image is surrounded by flames that rise through stems of vine and bramble with serpents coiled among them. At the top, left and right, two distraught angels hang suspended on the corners of the inner border.

Virginia Museum of Fine Arts Purchase, The Arthur and Margaret Glasgow Fund, 73.80.6/22

REFERENCE: Bindman 1987a, pp. 66–67 (text); pl. 5

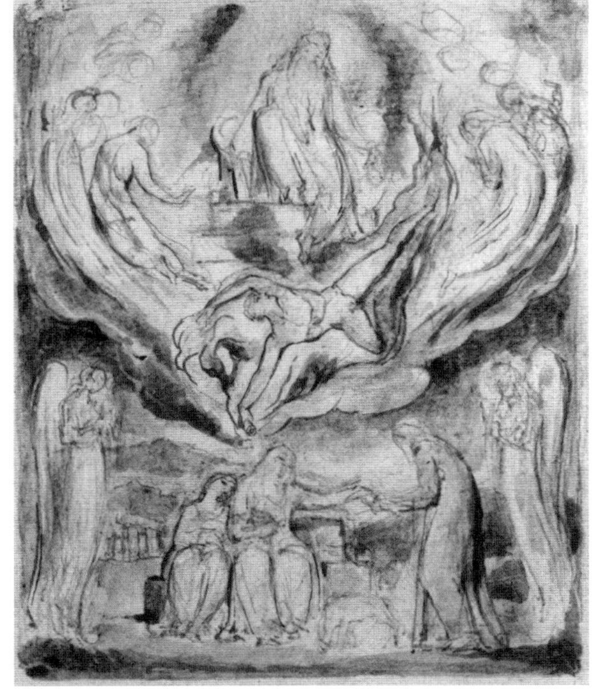

5A SATAN GOING FORTH FROM THE PRESENCE OF GOD CA. 1823
PENCIL, PEN, AND WATERCOLOR
3 1/4 X 4 3/16 INCHES (133 X 112 MM)

INSCRIBED 5, top right

The Syndics of the Fitzwilliam Museum, Cambridge, England, PD.31-1950

REFERENCE: Bindman 1970, p. 47, no. 39(7)

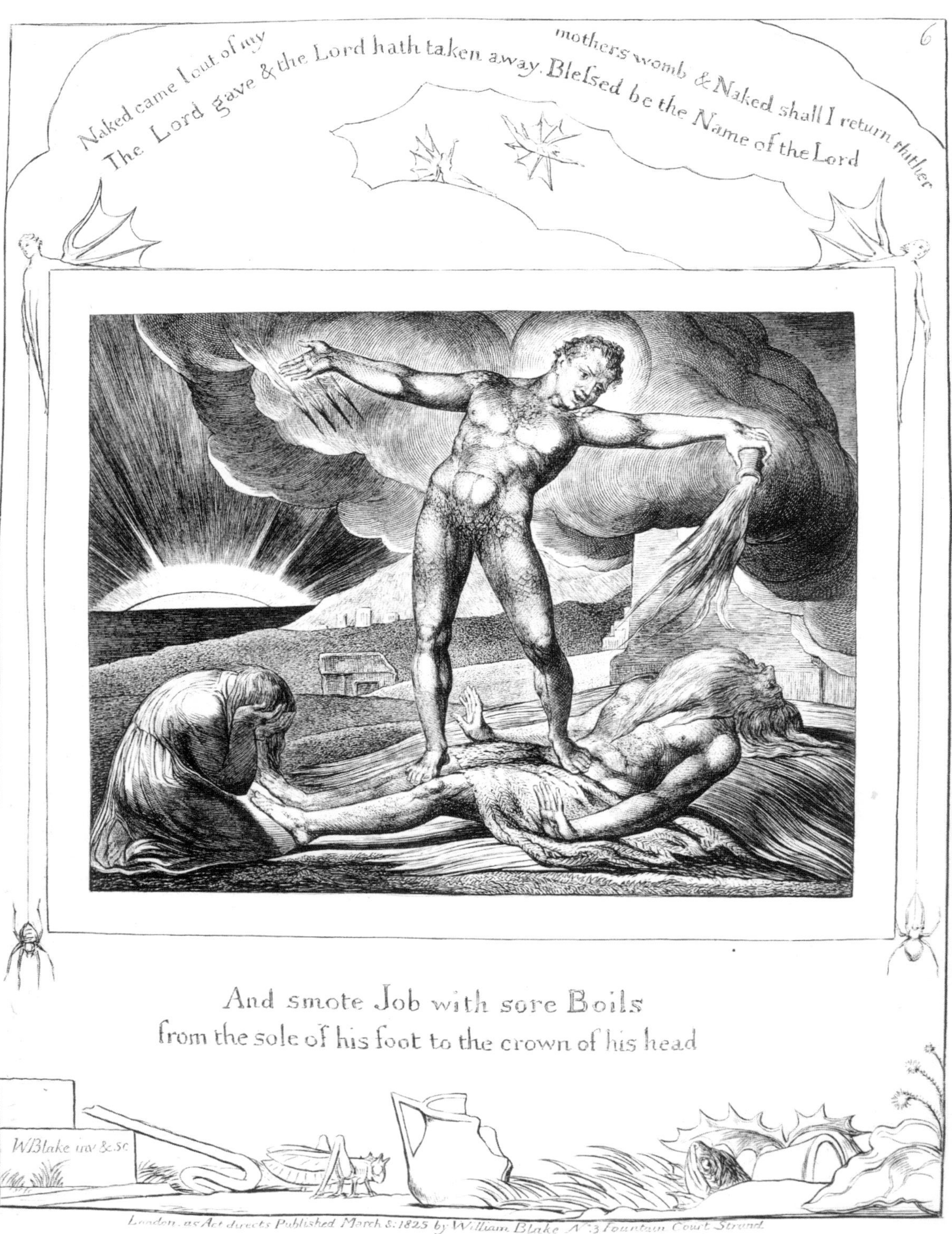
6
Naked came I out of my mothers womb & Naked shall I return thither
The Lord gave & the Lord hath taken away. Blessed be the Name of the Lord
And smote Job with sore Boils
from the sole of his foot to the crown of his head
W Blake inv & sc
London, as Act directs Published March 8: 1825 by William Blake N:3 Fountain Court Strand

PLATE 6

Satan Smiting Job with Boils

ENGRAVING; DESIGN 7 5/8 X 5 3/4 INCHES (194 X 147 MM)

INSCRIBED ABOVE THE IMAGE: *Naked came I out of my / mother's womb & Naked shall I return thither / The Lord gave & the Lord hath taken away. Blessed be the Name of the Lord* (JOB 1:21, USED IN THE ANGLICAN BURIAL SERVICE); BELOW THE IMAGE: *And smote Job with sore Boils / from the sole of his foot to the crown of his head* (JOB 2:7). SIGNED ON PLATE, LOWER LEFT, WITH PUBLISHER'S IMPRINT UNDERNEATH.

Satan, with a halo (making him, for Blake, the intermingling of God and Satan), stands on Job's abdomen and knee as he pours poisonous fluid from a phial held in his outstretched hand. Job arches his back in pain as he lies on a bed of straw, while his wife crouches in despair at his feet. Job seems to bear on his hand the marks of the stigmata (the crucifixion wounds of Jesus); his sufferings were seen by conventional Christian church teaching to prefigure the passion of Christ.

Blake may have taken this pose of Satan (which he first used in his print of *Glad Day*, 1780) from a figure in Vincenzo Scamozzi's *L'Idea dell' architettura universale* or from a bronze faun from Herculaneum, engraved in 1767–71, which Blake copied. All the details in the margins emphasize death, decay, and destruction, as Lindberg (1973) has pointed out. Blake has drawn images taken from the *Book of Job* and elsewhere in the Bible, for example, the spider's webs held by satanic ministers; the grass ("all flesh is as grass, and.... grass withereth," 1 PETER 1:24); the frog and the locust (EXODUS 8,10); the broken shepherd's crook; and the broken pot, a particular symbol of death. These images add to Job's feeling of despair over losing his material possessions.

Virginia Museum of Fine Arts Purchase, The Arthur and Margaret Glasgow Fund, 73.80.7/22

REFERENCE: Bindman 1987, pp. 64–66 (text); pl. 4

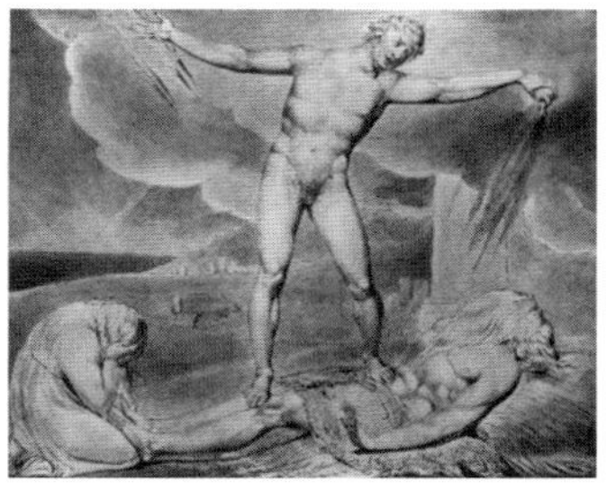

6A SATAN SMITING JOB WITH BOILS
(COLOR PLATE III) CA. 1804–7
PEN AND WATERCOLOR,
APPROXIMATELY 9 3/16 X 11 INCHES
(234 X 280 MM)

The Pierpont Morgan Library, New York, III, 45, PLATE 6

REFERENCE: Butlin 1981, p. 412, no. 550.6, pl. 702

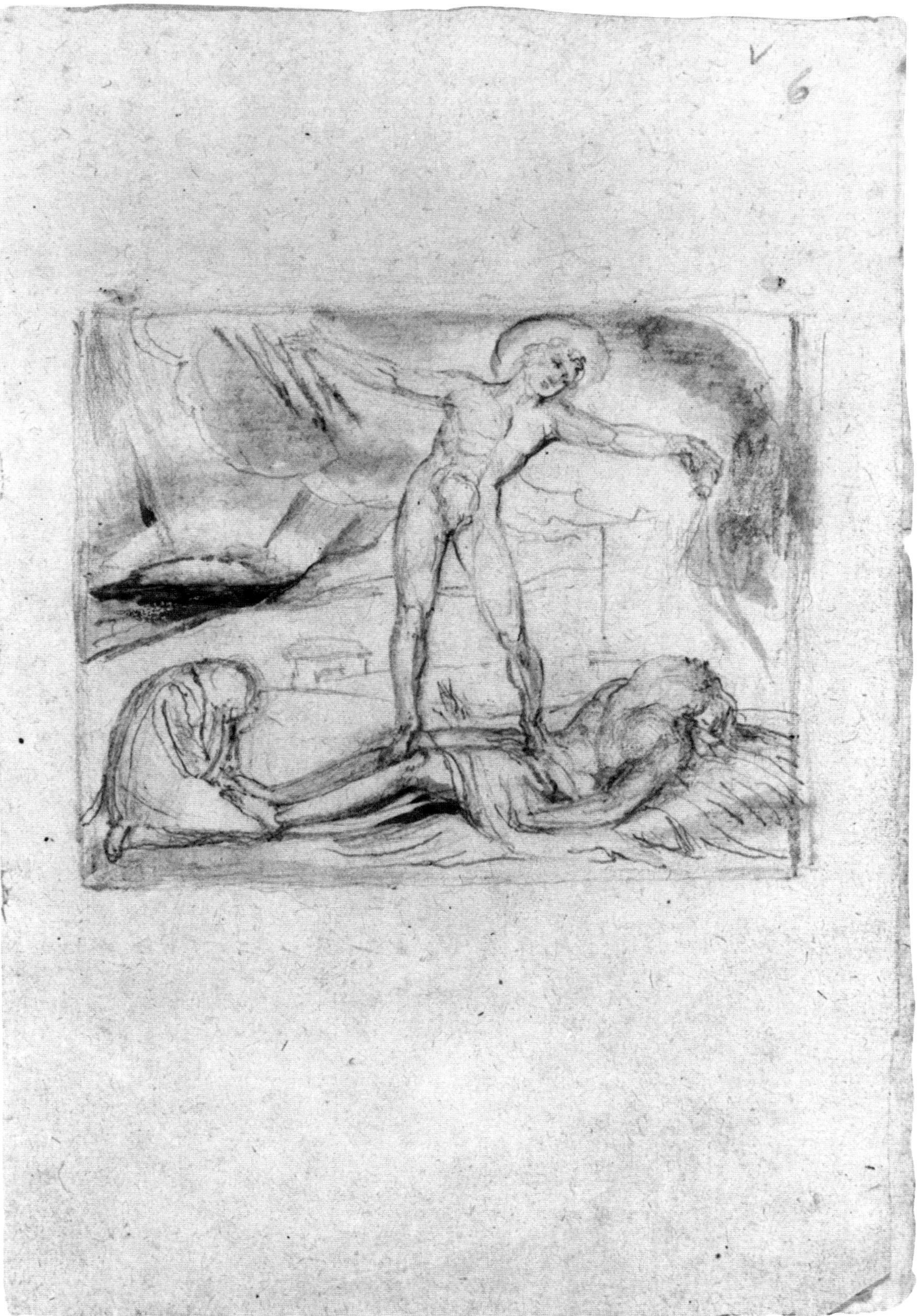

6B Satan Smiting Job with Boils ca. 1823
pencil, pen, india ink, and grey wash
$3\frac{13}{16}$ x $4\frac{9}{16}$ inches (97 x 115 mm)

inscribed 6, top right

The Syndics of the Fitzwilliam Museum, Cambridge, England, PD.32-1950

reference: Bindman 1970, p. 47, no. 39(8)

6C Satan Smiting Job with Boils ca. 1826
pencil and watercolor
$3\frac{3}{4}$ x $4\frac{7}{8}$ inches (96 x 123 mm)

Yale Center for British Art, New Haven, Paul Mellon Collection, B.1992.8.7(7)

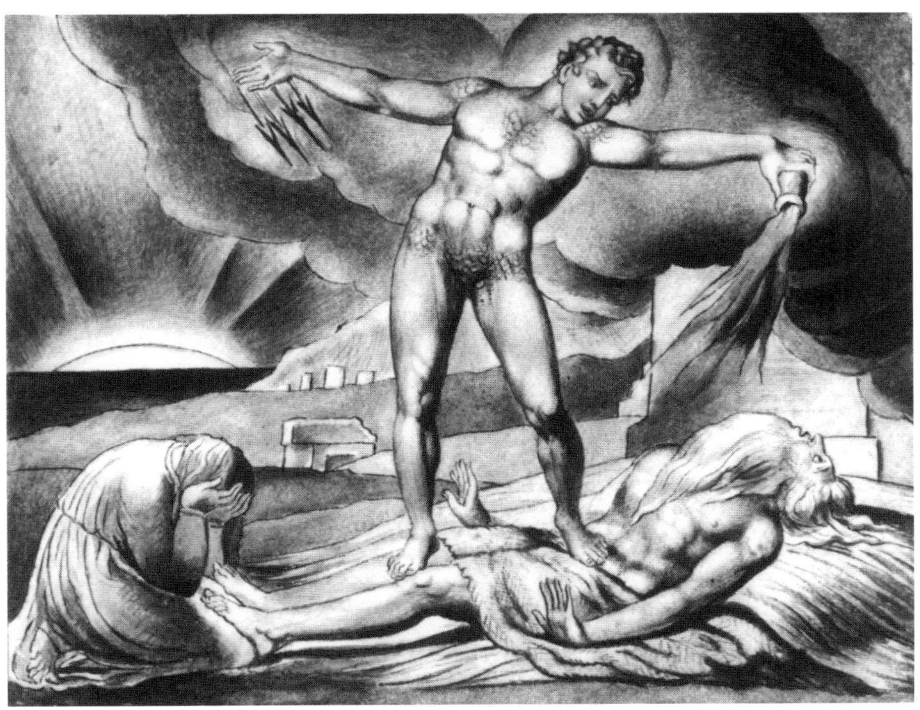

What! shall we recieve Good at the hand of God & shall we not also recieve Evil

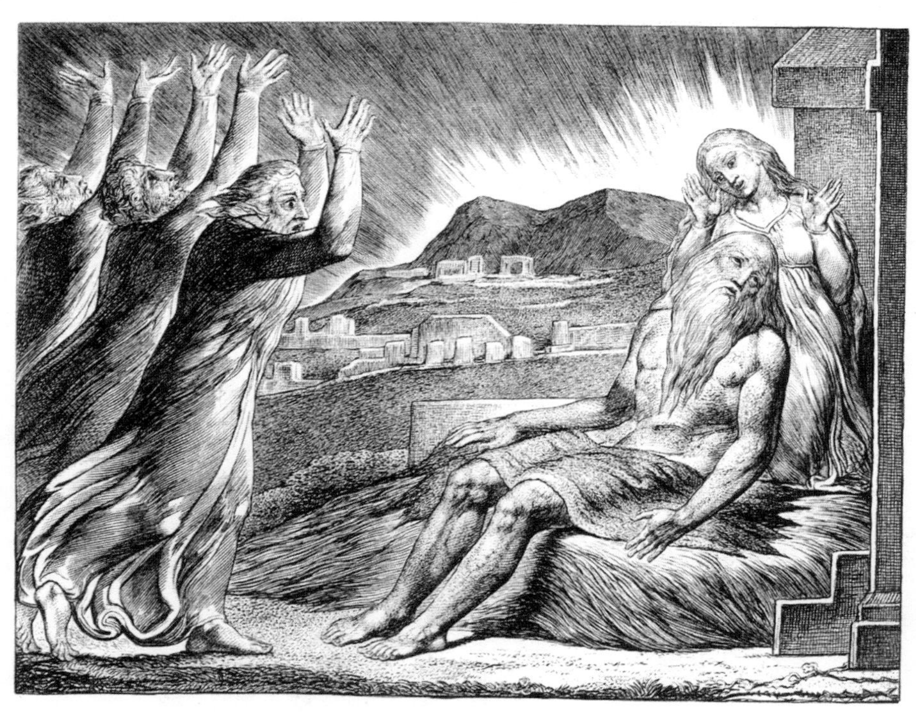

And when they lifted up their eyes afar off & knew him not they lifted up their voice & wept. & they rent every Man his mantle & sprinkled dust upon their heads towards heaven

Ye have heard of the Patience of Job and have seen the end of the Lord

W Blake inven & sculpt

London. Published as the Act directs March 8. 1825 by William Blake N3 Fountain Court Strand

PLATE 7

Job's Comforters

ENGRAVING; DESIGN 7 9/16 X 5 5/16 INCHES (192 X 151 MM)

INSCRIBED ABOVE THE IMAGE: *What! shall we recieve* [SIC] *Good / at the hand of God & shall we not also / recieve* [SIC] *Evil* (JOB 2:10); BELOW THE IMAGE: *And when they lifted up their eyes afar off & knew him not / they lifted up their voice & wept, & they rent every Man his / mantle & sprinkled dust upon their heads towards heaven* (JOB 2:12). SIGNED ON PLATE, BOTTOM RIGHT, WITH PUBLISHER'S IMPRINT UNDERNEATH.

The three friends were Eliphaz, the Temanite; Bildad, the Shuhite; and Zophar, the Naamathite, who see Job on a dung hill and lament his condition. The figures seated on the upper corners of the image appear to be weeping, and in the lower margins Job and his wife are downcast, Job with sheep at his feet and his wife with a sheep dog. Along the bottom margin is inscribed: *Ye have heard of the Patience of Job and have seen the end of the Lord* (JAMES 5: 11), another reference to Job's prefiguration of Christ. So far Job has endured his trials.

There are other Christian references in the imagery: the echo of Michelangelo's *Pietà* in the principal figures of Job and his wife, and the suggestion of a cross in the architecture at the right.

Virginia Museum of Fine Arts Purchase, The Arthur and Margaret Glasgow Fund, 73.80.5/22

REFERENCE: Bindman 1987a, pp. 69–70 (text); pl. 7

7A JOB'S COMFORTERS CA. 1823
PENCIL, PEN, AND WASH
3 5/8 X 4 1/2 INCHES (92 X 114 MM)

INSCRIBED *7*, top right

The Syndics of the Fitzwilliam Museum, Cambridge, England, PD.33-1950

REFERENCE: Bindman 1970, pp. 47-48, no. 39(9)

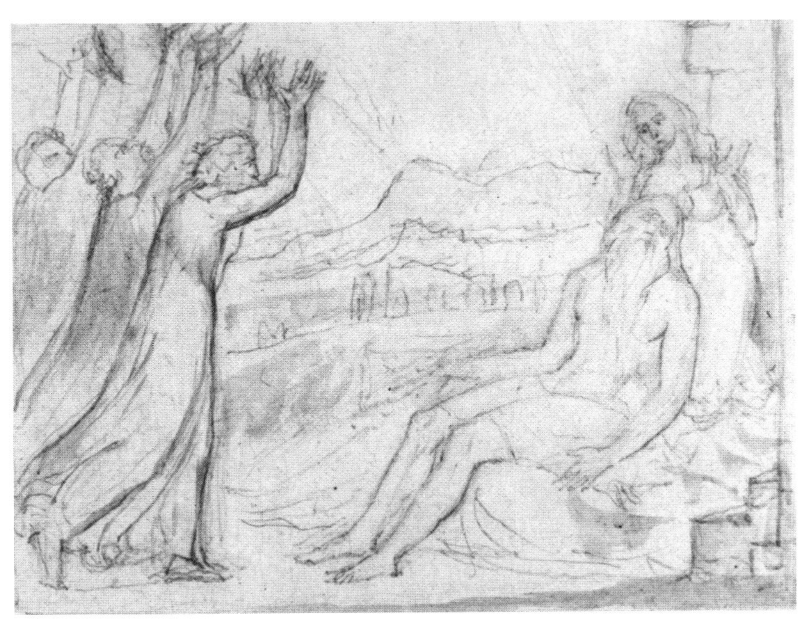

Lo let that night be solitary
& let no joyful voice come therein

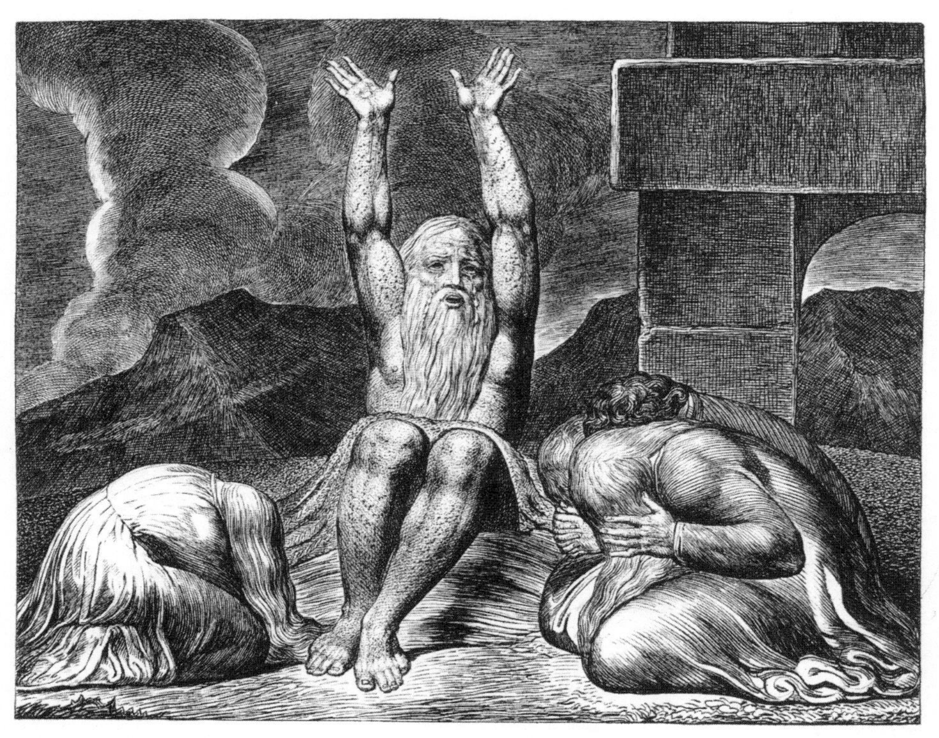

Let the Day perish wherein I was Born

And they sat down with him upon the ground seven days & seven nights & none spake a word unto him for they saw that his grief was very great

W Blake inv & sculp

London Publish'd as the Act directs March 8: 1825 by Will.m Blake N.o 3 Fountain Court Strand

PLATE 8

Job's Despair

ENGRAVING; DESIGN 7 1/2 X 5 3/8 INCHES (191 X 149 MM)

INSCRIBED ABOVE THE IMAGE: *Lo let that night be solitary / & let no joyful voice come therein* (JOB 3:7); BELOW THE IMAGE: *Let the Day perish wherein I was Born* (JOB 3:3) / *And they sat down with him upon the ground seven days & seven / nights & none spake a word unto him for they saw that his grief / was very great* (JOB 2:13). SIGNED ON PLATE, LOWER RIGHT, WITH PUBLISHER'S IMPRINT UNDERNEATH.

Satan's work seems finally to have succeeded. Job's patience has ended and he curses the day he was born. The traditional iconography of Job, as in plate 7, usually emphasizes his stoicism; here Blake follows the biblical account of Job very closely, but at the same time sets the stage for his own interpretation in which Job's despair gives way to a spiritual belief in the power of imagination. The lower border with its images of toadstools, brambles, and thistles emphasizes the desolation.

Virginia Museum of Fine Arts Purchase, The Arthur and Margaret Glasgow Fund, 73.80.9/22

REFERENCE: Bindman 1987a, pp. 70–72 (text); see also Plate 8.

8A JOB'S DESPAIR CA. 1823
PENCIL, PEN, AND WATERCOLOR
3 1/2 X 4 3/4 INCHES (89 X 120 MM)

INSCRIBED *8*, top right

The Syndics of the Fitzwilliam Museum, Cambridge, England, PD.34-1950

REFERENCE: Bindman 1970, p. 48, no. 39(10)

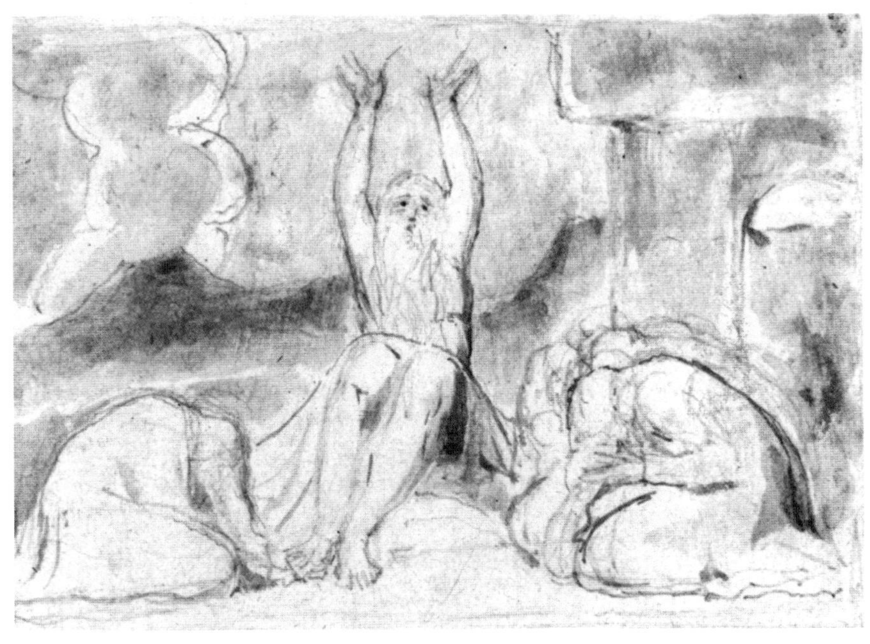

Shall mortal Man be more Just than God? Shall a Man be more Pure than his Maker? Behold he putteth no trust in his Saints & his Angels he chargeth with folly

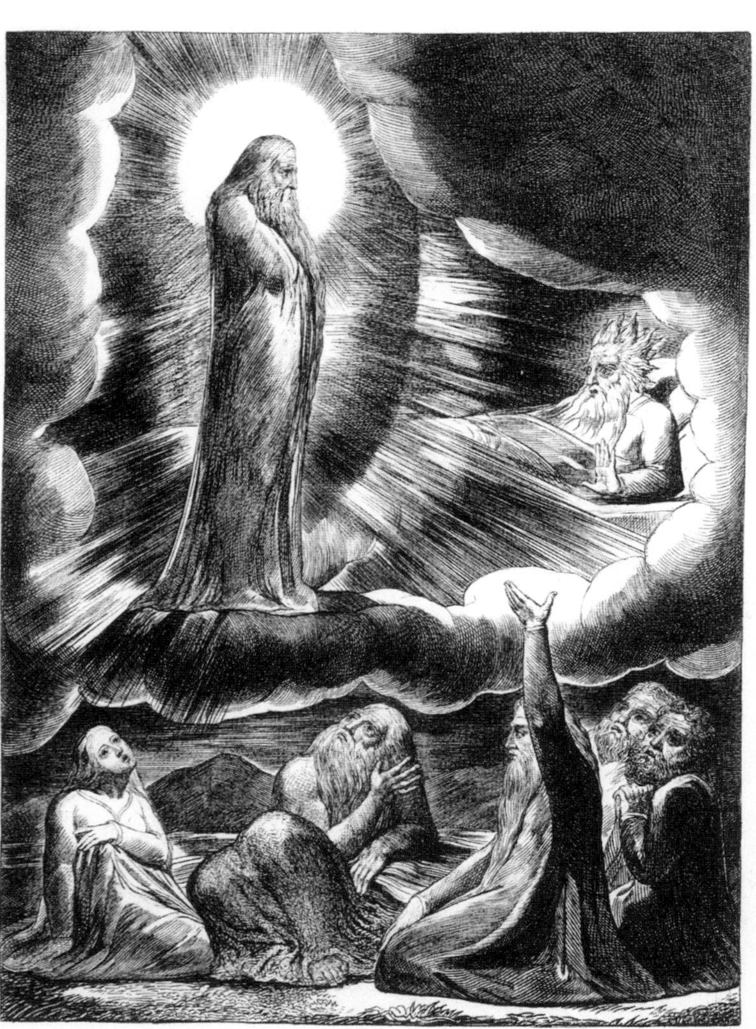

Then a Spirit passed before my face
the hair of my flesh stood up

W Blake invenit & sculp

London, Published as the Act directs March 8: 1825 by William Blake No. 3 Fountain Court Strand

PLATE 9

The Vision of Eliphaz

ENGRAVING; DESIGN 7 9/16 X 5 5/8 INCHES (193 X 143 MM)

INSCRIBED ABOVE THE IMAGE ARE GOD'S WORDS TO ELIPHAZ: *Shall mortal Man be more Just than God? Shall a Man be more Pure than / his Maker? Behold he putteth no trust in his Saints & his Angels he chargeth with Folly* (JOB 4:17–18); BELOW THE IMAGE, ELIPHAZ'S ACCOUNT OF GOD'S APPEARANCE: *Then a Spirit passed before my face / the hair of my flesh stood up* (JOB 4:15). SIGNED ON PLATE LOWER RIGHT MARGIN, WITH PUBLISHER'S IMPRINT UNDERNEATH.

Eliphaz points to his vision and tries to help Job by persuading him of its terrifying truth: How dare Job, as a mere mortal, criticize God? This was the old, traditional view of God. For Blake, however, man was immortal and could commune with God through the power of his artistic imagination.

In the margins, clouds containing Blake's inscriptions drift above the interlaced boughs of leafless trees.

Virginia Museum of Fine Arts Purchase, The Arthur and Margaret Glasgow Fund, 73.80.10/22

REFERENCE: Bindman 1987a, pp. 72–73 (text); pl. 9

9A THE VISION OF ELIPHAZ CA. 1823
PENCIL, PEN, INDIA INK, AND WATERCOLOR
5 1/2 X 3 9/16 INCHES (139 X 90 MM)

INSCRIBED 9, top right

The Syndics of the Fitzwilliam Museum, Cambridge, England, PD.35-1950

REFERENCES: Bindman 1970, p. 48, no. 39(11)

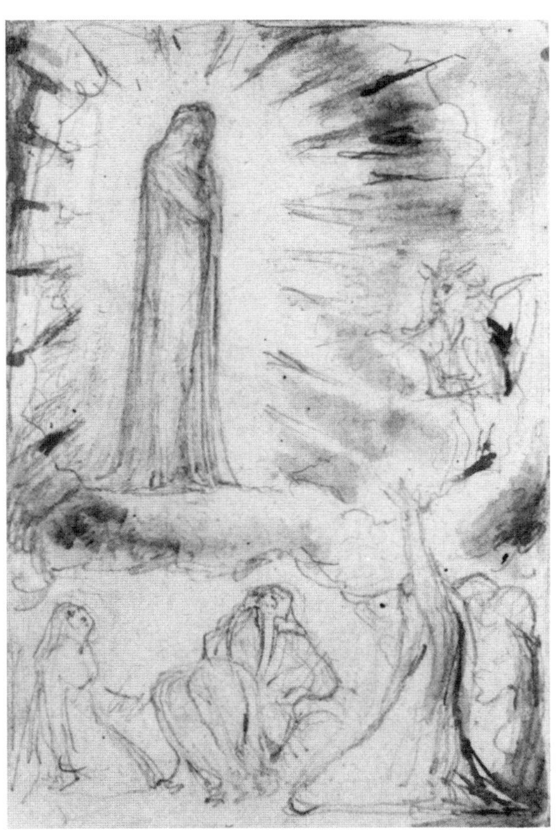

But he knoweth the way that I take
when he hath tried me I shall come forth like gold

Have pity upon me! Have pity upon me. O ye my friends
for the hand of God hath touched me

Though he slay me yet will I trust in him

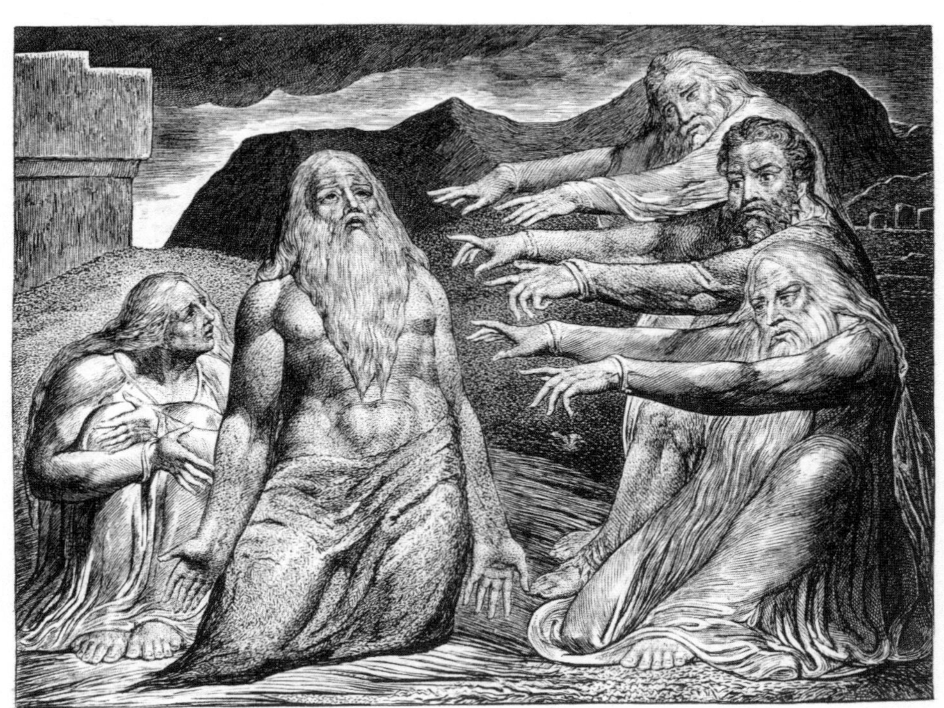

The Just Upright Man is laughed to scorn

Man that is born of a Woman is of few days & full of trouble
he cometh up like a flower & is cut down he fleeth also as a shadow
& continueth not. And dost thou open thine eyes upon such a one
& bringest me into judgment with thee

W Blake invenit & sculp

London Published as the Act directs March 8: 1825 by William Blake N 3 Fountain Court Strand

PLATE 10

Job Rebuked by His Friends

ENGRAVING; DESIGN 7 5/8 X 5 7/8 INCHES (193 X 150 MM)

INSCRIBED ABOVE THE IMAGE: *But he knoweth the way that I take / when he hath tried me I shall come forth like gold* (JOB 23: 10) / *Have pity upon me! Have pity upon me! O ye my friends / for the hand of God hath touched me* (JOB 19:21; THESE WORDS ACTUALLY COME BEFORE ELIPHAZ'S VISION, BUT ARE PART OF JOB'S LONG COMPLAINT AGAINST GOD) / *Though he slay me yet will I trust in him* (JOB 13:15); BELOW THE IMAGE: *The Just Upright Man is laughed to scorn* (JOB 12:4) / *Man that is born of a Woman is of few days & full of trouble / he cometh up like a flower & is cut down he fleeth also as a shadow / & continueth not. And dost thou open thine eyes upon such a one / & bringest me into judgment with thee* (JOB 14:1–3; ALSO USED IN ANGLICAN BURIAL SERVICE). SIGNED ON PLATE, LOWER RIGHT MARGIN, WITH PUBLISHER'S IMPRINT UNDERNEATH. WATERMARK: *J WHATMAN 1825.*

Job, with spotted skin and a sackcloth around his waist, is taunted by his friends, who seem to have lost patience with his denunciation of God; even his wife seems to be reproaching him. The scene can be interpreted as a prefiguration of the Mocking of Christ. The striking image of the pointing figures may have been taken from Fuseli's *The Three Witches.* Blunt (1959) suggests that both Blake and Fuseli had a common source in Perino del Vaga's *The Fall of the Giants* (engraved by Enea Vico), but according to Lindberg (1973) its older source could equally well be Giulio Romano's *The Adoration of the Shepherds*, engraved by Agostino Venziano in 1521. In the bottom left-hand corner a raven(?) tramples on a serpent; on the right, an owl grasps a mouse. At the top are two figures dragged down by chains.

Virginia Museum of Fine Arts Purchase, The Arthur and Margaret Glasgow Fund, 73.80.11/22

REFERENCE: Bindman 1987a, pp. 73–75 (text); pl. 10

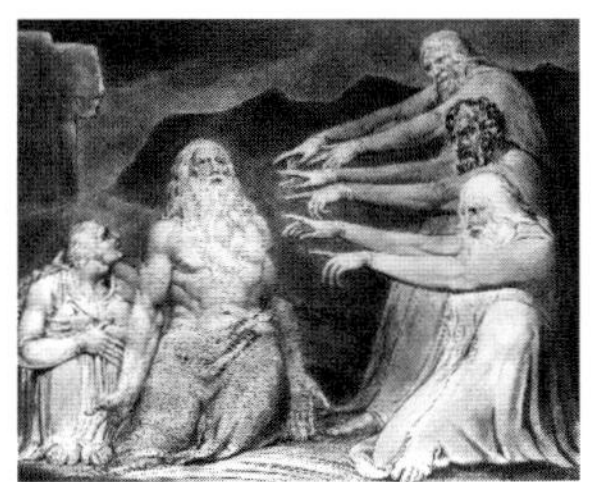

10A JOB REBUKED BY HIS FRIENDS CA. 1804–7
(COLOR PLATE IV)
PEN AND WATERCOLOR
9 3/16 X 11 INCHES (234 X 280 MM)

SIGNED ON PLATE: *WB inv.*, lower right.

Developed from Blake's large engraving published in 1793 and entitled *Job.*

The Pierpont Morgan Library, New York, III, 45, PLATE 10

REFERENCE: Butlin 1981, p. 413, no. 550.10, pl. 706

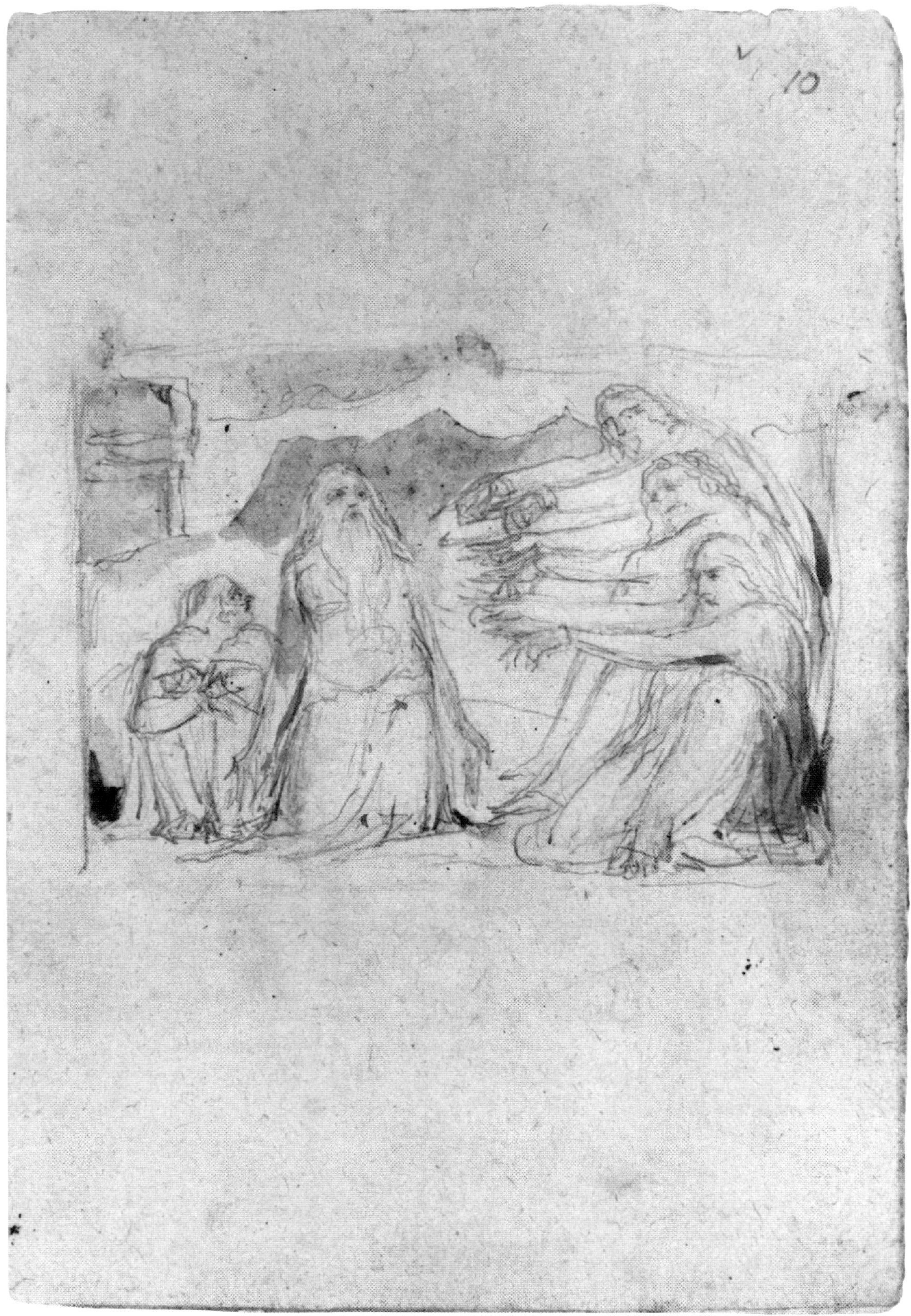

10B Job Rebuked by His Friends ca. 1823
pencil, ink, and watercolor
3 1/2 x 4 7/8 inches (89 x 124 mm)
inscribed *10*, top right
The Syndics of the Fitzwilliam Museum, Cambridge, England, PD.36-1950
reference: Bindman 1970, p. 48, no. 39(12)

10C Job Rebuked by His Friends ca. 1826
pencil and watercolor
3 5/8 x 4 3/4 inches (93 x 121 mm)
Yale Center for British Art, New Haven, Paul Mellon Collection, B.1992.8.7(11)
reference: Bindman 1987a, pl. 10c; 1987b, 1:15; 2: pl. 10

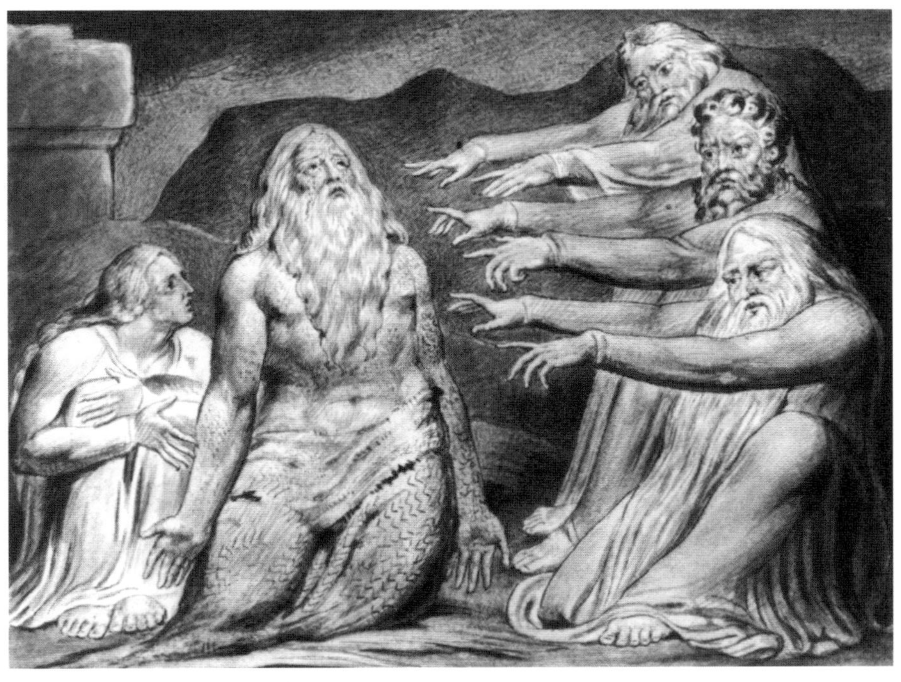

My bones are pierced in me in the night season & my sinews take no rest

My skin is black upon me & my bones are burned with heat

The triumphing of the wicked is short, the joy of the hypocrite is but for a moment

Satan himself is transformed into an Angel of Light & his Ministers into Ministers of Righteousness

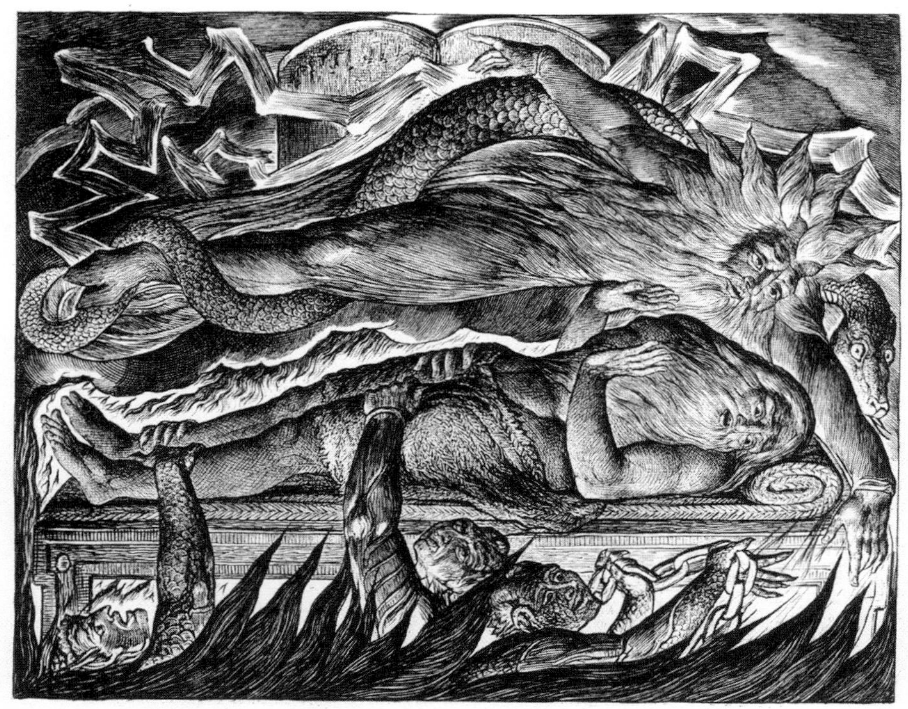

With Dreams upon my bed thou scarest me & affrightest me with Visions

Why do you persecute me as God & are not satisfied with my flesh. Oh that my words were printed in a Book that they were graven with an iron pen & lead in the rock for ever For I know that my Redeemer liveth & that he shall stand in the latter days upon the Earth & after my skin destroy thou This body yet in my flesh shall I see God whom I shall see for Myself and mine eyes shall behold & not Another tho consumed be my wrought Image

Who opposeth & exalteth himself above all that is called God or is Worshipped

W Blake invenit & sculp

London. Published as the Act directs March 8: 1825 by Willm Blake N° 3 Fountain Court Strand

PLATE 11

Job's Evil Dreams

ENGRAVING; DESIGN AREA 7 9/16 X 5 5/8 INCHES (192 X 146 MM)

INSCRIBED ABOVE THE IMAGE, ON THE LEFT: *My bones are pierced in me in the / night season & my sinews / take no rest* (JOB 30:17); ON THE RIGHT: *My skin is black upon me / & my bones are burned / with heat* (JOB 30:30); IN THE MIDDLE: *The triumphing of the wicked / is short, the joy of the hypocrite is / but for a moment* (JOB 20:5); AND ALONG TOP EDGE OF IMAGE: *Satan himself is transformed into an Angel of Light & his Ministers into Ministers of Righteousness* (2 CORINTHIANS, 11:14-15, ABBREVIATED). BELOW THE IMAGE: *With Dreams upon my bed thou scarest me & affrightest me / with Visions* (ALTERED VERSION OF JOB 7:14) */ Why do you persecute me as God & are not satisfied with my flesh. Oh that my words / were printed in a Book that they were graven with an iron pen & lead in the rock for ever / For I know that my Redeemer liveth & that he shall stand in the latter days upon / the Earth & after my skin destroy thou This body yet in my flesh shall I see God / whom I shall see for Myself and mine eyes shall behold & not Another tho consumed be my wrought Image* (JOB 19:22-27, JOB'S ANSWER TO BILDAD, SLIGHTLY CHANGED, ALSO NOW IN ANGLICAN BURIAL SERVICE) */ Who opposeth & exalteth himself above all that is called God or is Worshipped* (2 THESSALONIANS 2:4). SIGNED ON PLATE, BOTTOM LEFT, WITH PUBLISHER'S IMPRINT UNDERNEATH.

Satan, disguised as God but betrayed by his cloven hoof and the serpent wrapped around it, points with one hand to tablets of law that bear indecipherable Hebrew words, and with the other hand to the sufferings of Hell. A scaly devil awaits Job, chains in hand, while two others clutch at him from the depths. This horrific nightmare is Job's lowest point.

It can also be seen as the turning point. Job now recognizes that by adhering too closely to the letter of the law, which Satan/God as an impostor has been foolish enough to reveal, he had failed to realize that man is also immortal: *I know that my Redeemer liveth* (used so gloriously by Handel in *The Messiah*). The figure of Satan with outstretched arms was used more than once by Blake in, for example, *The Lazar House* and *Hervey's Meditations*, as well as by Fuseli, Flaxman, and George Romney. All of these artists ultimately based their interpretations on an image of Jupiter Pluvius from the ancient column to Marcus Aurelius in Rome.

In Christian terms the afflictions of Job are an allegory of the sufferings of humans in Hell (Lindberg 1973), as well as those of Christ.

Virginia Museum of Fine Arts Purchase, The Arthur and Margaret Glasgow Fund, 73.80.12/22

REFERENCE: Bindman 1987a, pp. 75–77 (text); pl. 11

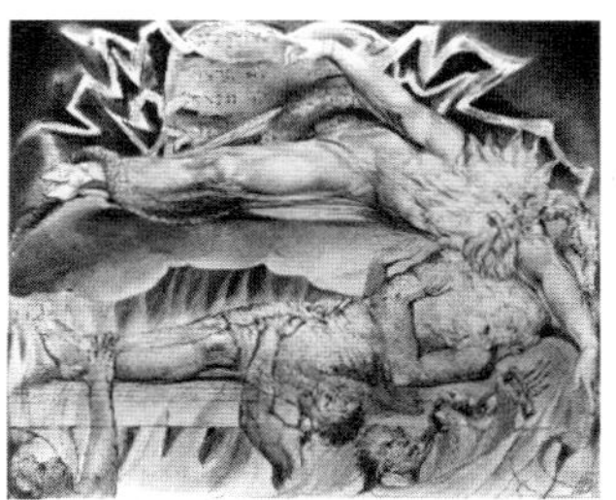

11A JOB'S EVIL DREAMS CA. 1804–7
(COLOR PLATE V)
PEN AND WATERCOLOR
9 5/16 X 11 5/16 INCHES (237 X 288 MM)
INSCRIBED IN HEBREW: Tables of the Law, excerpts from the Ten Commandments (EXODUS 20: 12–15), and signed, lower right: *WB inv.*
The Pierpont Morgan Library, New York, III, 45, PLATE 11
REFERENCE: Butlin 1981, p. 414, no. 550.11, pl. 107

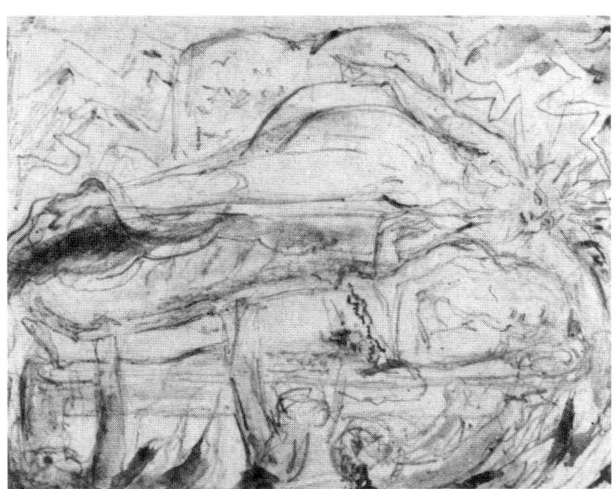

11B JOB'S EVIL DREAMS CA. 1823
PENCIL, PEN, INDIA INK, AND WATERCOLOR
3 5/8 X 4 5/8 INCHES (92 X 117 MM)
INSCRIBED *11*, top right
The Syndics of the Fitzwilliam Museum, Cambridge, England, PD.37-1950
REFERENCE: Bindman 1970, p. 48, no. 39(13)

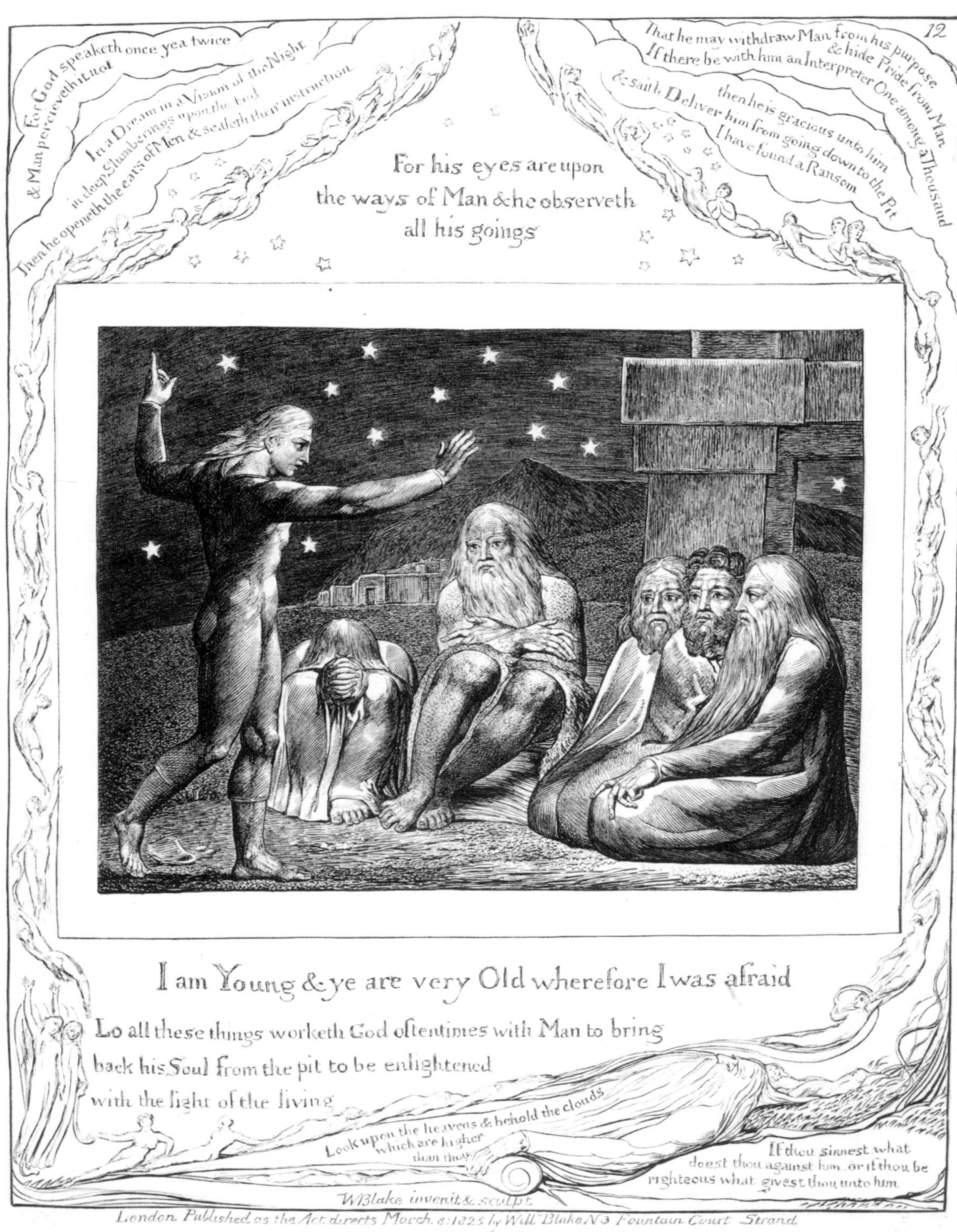
12
For God speaketh once yea twice
& Man perceiveth it not
In a Dream in a Vision of the Night
in deep Slumberings upon the bed
Then he openeth the ears of Men & sealeth their instruction
That he may withdraw Man from his purpose
& hide Pride from Man
If there be with him an Interpreter One among a Thousand
then he is gracious unto him
& saith Deliver him from going down to the Pit
I have found a Ransom
For his eyes are upon
the ways of Man & he observeth
all his goings
I am Young & ye are very Old wherefore I was afraid
Lo all these things worketh God oftentimes with Man to bring
back his Soul from the pit to be enlightened
with the light of the living
Look upon the heavens & behold the clouds
which are higher
than thou
If thou sinnest what
doest thou against him or if thou be
righteous what givest thou unto him
W Blake invenit & sculpt
London Published as the Act directs March 8:1825 by Willm Blake N 3 Fountain Court Strand

PLATE 12
The Wrath of Elihu

ENGRAVING; DESIGN 7 1/2 X 5 11/16 INCHES (191 X 147 MM)

INSCRIBED ABOVE THE IMAGE, ON THE LEFT: *For God speaketh once yea twice / & Man percieveth* [SIC] *it not / In a Dream in a Vision of the Night / in deep Slumberings upon the bed / Then he openeth the ears of Men & sealeth their instruction* (JOB 33:14-16); ON THE RIGHT: *That he may withdraw Man from his purpose / & hide Pride from Man* (JOB 33:17)/ *If there be with him an Interpreter One among a Thousand / then he is gracious unto him / & saith Deliver him from going down to the Pit / I have found a Ransom* (JOB 33: 23-24); AND IN THE MIDDLE: *For his eyes are upon / the ways of Man & he observeth / all his goings* (JOB 34:21). BELOW THE IMAGE: *I am Young & ye are very Old wherefore I was afraid* (JOB 32:6); *Lo all these things worketh God oftentimes with Man to bring / back his Soul from the pit to be enlightened / with the light of the living* (JOB 33:29-30); *Look upon the heavens and behold the clouds / which are higher / than thou; If thou sinnest, what / doest thou against him or if thou be / righteous what givest thou unto him* (JOB 35:5-7). SIGNED ON PLATE, BOTTOM CENTER, WITH PUBLISHER'S IMPRINT UNDERNEATH.

In this dramatic image the young Elihu is moved to lecture Job that divine vision is the chief instructor of men, that God is not interested in the righteousness of men, and that the Interpreter (Christ) will raise man from the pit (death) to be illuminated with the light of the living. As Job and his friends listen attentively, and his wife prays, the stars shine out and the worst is over (Lindberg 1973, pp. 272–3). In the margin what appear to be the dreams of Job as a law-abiding moralist ascend to meet the stars. At the upper left, between the stream of embodied dreams and the clouds, is the constellation Orion, while at the right are the Pleiades. The figure of Elihu was taken from Raphael's *Blinding of Elymas.* Blake also seems to have made use of studies in physiognomy by Charles Le Brun (1619–1690), particularly, *Attention* for Elihu, *Scorn* for Eliphaz at right, and *Esteem* for Job.

Virginia Museum of Fine Arts Purchase, The Arthur and Margaret Glasgow Fund, 73.80.13/22

REFERENCE: Bindman 1987, pp. 77–78 (text); pl. 12

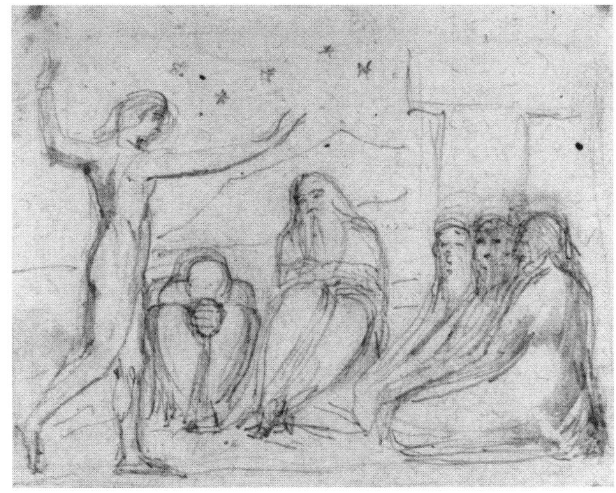

12A THE WRATH OF ELIHU CA. 1823
PENCIL, PEN, AND GREY WASH
3 5/8 X 4 7/8 INCHES (92 X 124 MM)
INSCRIBED *12*, top right
The Syndics of the Fitzwilliam Museum, Cambridge, England, PD.38-1950
REFERENCE: Bindman 1970, p. 48, no. 39(14)

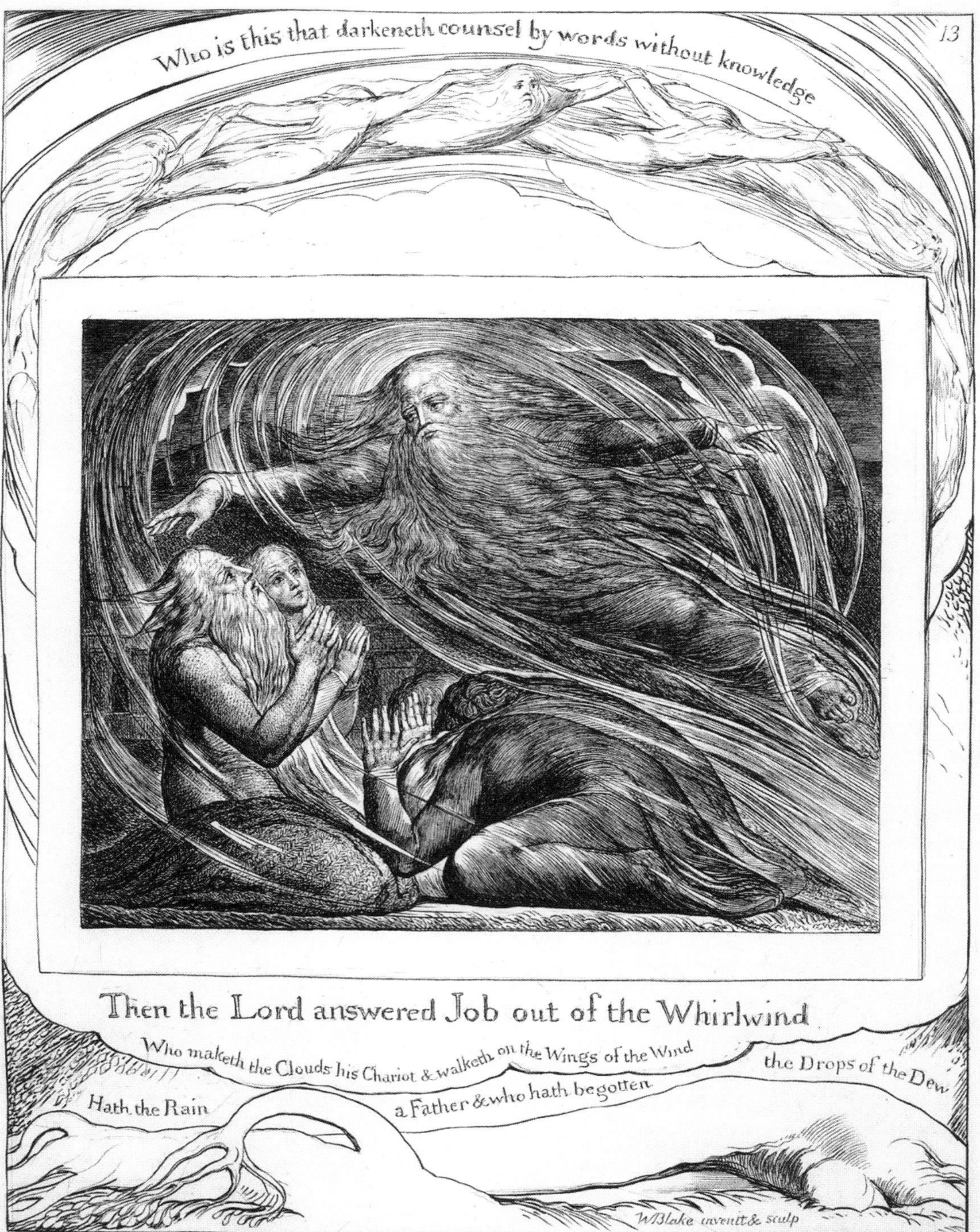
13
Who is this that darkeneth counsel by words without knowledge
Then the Lord answered Job out of the Whirlwind
Who maketh the Clouds his Chariot & walketh on the Wings of the Wind
the Drops of the Dew
Hath the Rain
a Father & who hath begotten
W Blake invenit & sculp
London Published as the Act directs March 8:1825 by William Blake No 3 Fountain Court Strand

PLATE 13

The Lord Answering Job out of a Whirlwind

ENGRAVING; DESIGN 7 5/8 X 5 3/4 INCHES (194 X 146 MM)

INSCRIBED ABOVE THE IMAGE: *Who is this that darkeneth counsel by words without knowledge* (JOB 38:2); BELOW THE IMAGE: *Then the Lord answered Job out of the Whirlwind* (JOB 38:1); / *Who maketh the Clouds his Chariot & walketh on the Wings of the Wind* (PSALM 104:3); AND *Hath the Rain / a Father & who hath begotten / the Drops of the Dew* (JOB 38:28). SIGNED ON PLATE BOTTOM RIGHT, WITH PUBLISHER'S IMPRINT UNDERNEATH.

This image is Job's first vision of the true God, who reminds Job of His powers. The insight that God is in everything, including human beings, is finally revealed to Job and his wife, but not to his friends, who cannot rise and cannot see God. This powerful revelation comes in a whirlwind that bends the trees in the margin.

Virginia Museum of Fine Arts Purchase, The Arthur and Margaret Glasgow Fund, 73.80.14/22

REFERENCE: Bindman 1987a, pp. 78–80 (text); pl. 13

13A THE LORD ANSWERING JOB OUT OF THE WHIRLWIND CA. 1823
PENCIL, PEN, AND WASH
3 7/8 X 4 1/2 INCHES (99 X 114 MM)

INSCRIBED *13*, top right

The Syndics of the Fitzwilliam Museum, Cambridge, England, PD.39-1950

REFERENCE: Bindman 1970, p. 48, no. 39(15)

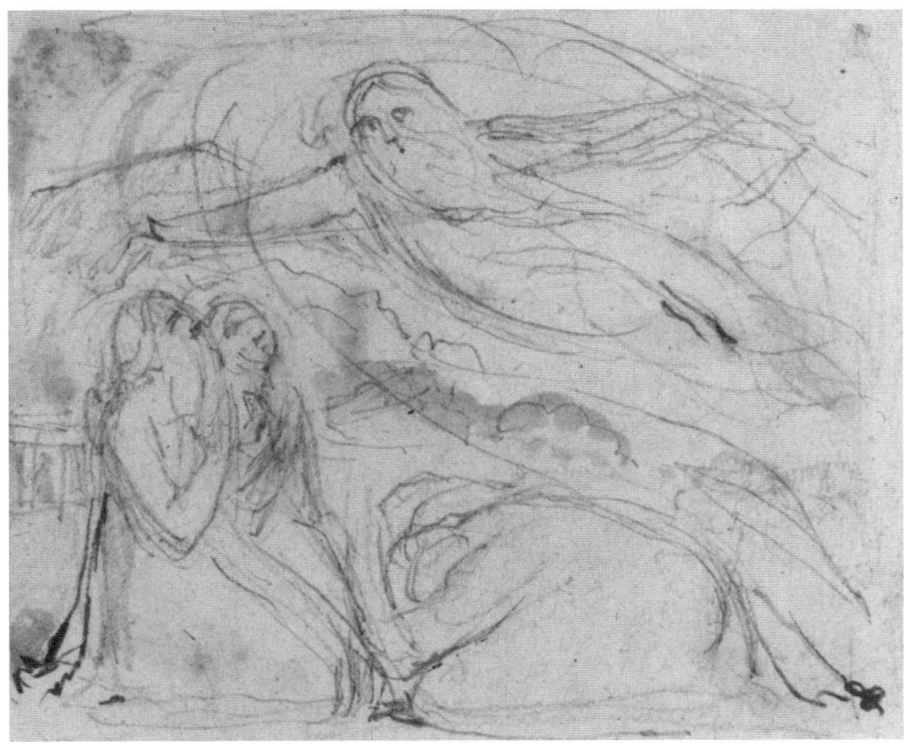

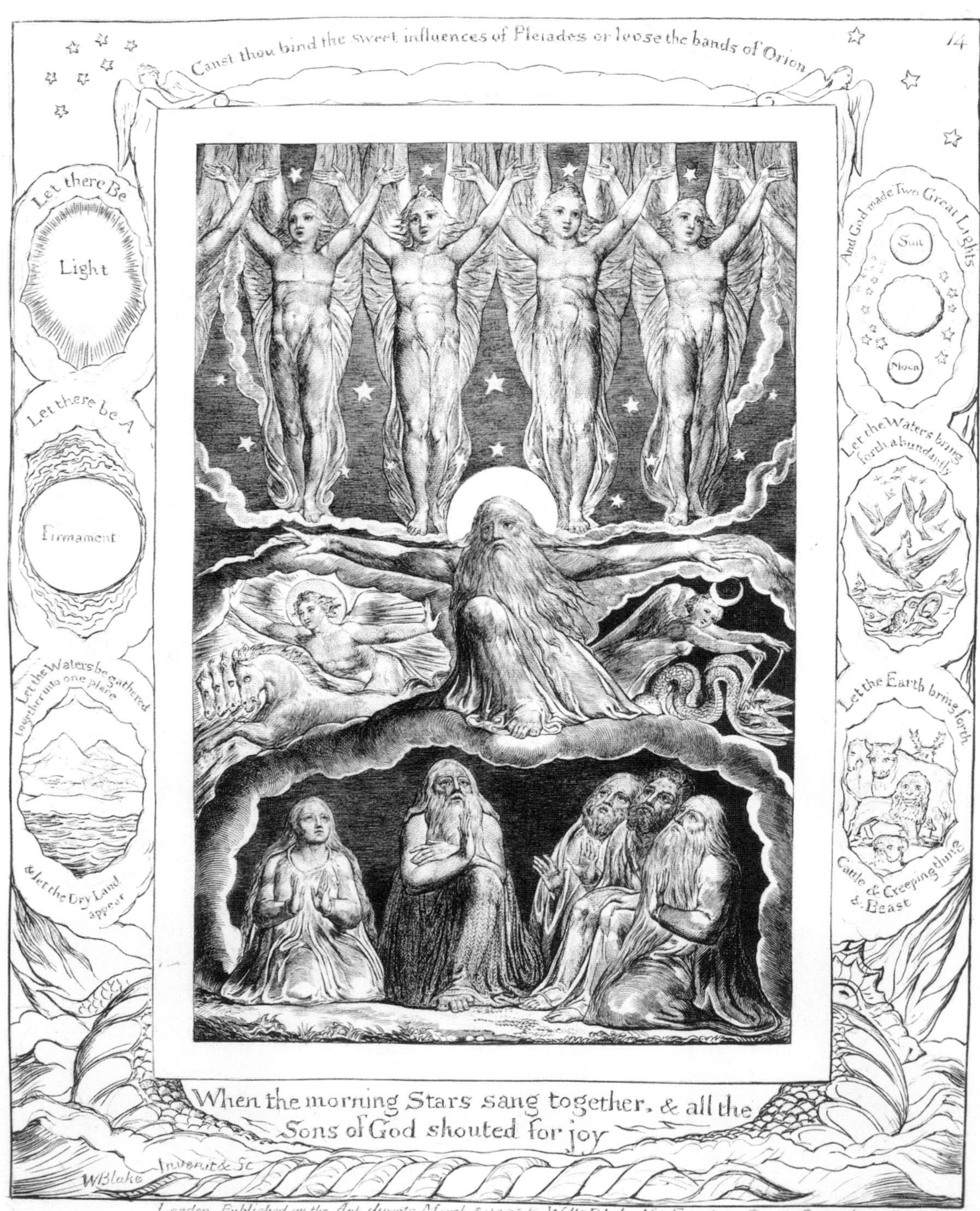

London. Published as the Act directs March 8:1825 by Willm Blake N3 Fountain Court Strand

PLATE 14

When the Morning Stars Sang Together

ENGRAVING; DESIGN 7 7/16 X 5 13/16 INCHES (189 X 148 MM)

INSCRIBED ABOVE THE IMAGE: *Canst thou bind the sweet influences of Pleiades or loose the bands of Orion* (JOB 38:31; SEE PLATE 12); AND BELOW THE IMAGE: *When the morning Stars sang together, & all the / Sons of God shouted for joy* (JOB 38:7). DOWN THE LEFT-HAND MARGIN: *Let there Be / Light* (GENESIS 1:3); *Let there be A / Firmament* (GENESIS 1:6); *Let the waters be gathered / together into one place / & let the Dry Land / appear* (GENESIS 1:9). DOWN THE RIGHT-HAND MARGIN: *And God made Two Great Lights / Sun / Moon* (GENESIS 1:16); *Let the Waters bring / forth abundantly* (GENESIS 1:20); *Let the Earth bring forth / Cattle & Creeping thing / & Beast* (GENESIS 1:24). SIGNED ON PLATE, LOWER LEFT, WITH PUBLISHER'S IMPRINT UNDERNEATH.

This image is the first of three visions (plates 14, 15, and 16) in which, as Lindberg (1973) points out, God reveals his powers. God asks, in a series of rhetorical questions, "Where wast thou when I laid the foundations of the earth?" (JOB 38: 4) and "When the morning Stars sang together, and all the sons of God shouted for joy." At God's right is the Greek sun god Helios with his four-horse chariot, who pushes away the clouds; to his left Selene with her moon diadem drives out two serpents. Their poses are derived from antique gems. Above are angels and stars, which Blake saw as interchangeable. Orion and the Pleiades are mentioned in the text above. God's halo, which is not engraved, is brighter than the Sun's, which is lightly stippled.

Beneath, in a cave, sit Job, his wife, and his friends (from right to left, Eliphaz, Bildad, and Zophar), separated from God by clouds, and prevented, too, from hearing the celestial music, the music of the spheres. In the margins are the six days of creation, while beneath, in fiery waters, are Leviathan and a huge worm entwined around a log. Blake has combined classical and biblical allusions for, as he wrote in *The Laocoön*, "The Gods of Priam are the Cherubim of Moses and Salomon: the Hosts of Heaven." Eventually, Job and his wife may be able to comprehend the eternity of God's creation, as Blake's hieroglyph in the preliminary drawing from the Fitzwilliam seems to suggest (SEE NO. 14A).

Virginia Museum of Fine Arts Purchase, The Arthur and Margaret Glasgow Fund, 73.80.15/22

REFERENCE: Bindman 1987a, pp. 80–82 (text); pl. 14

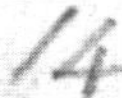

14

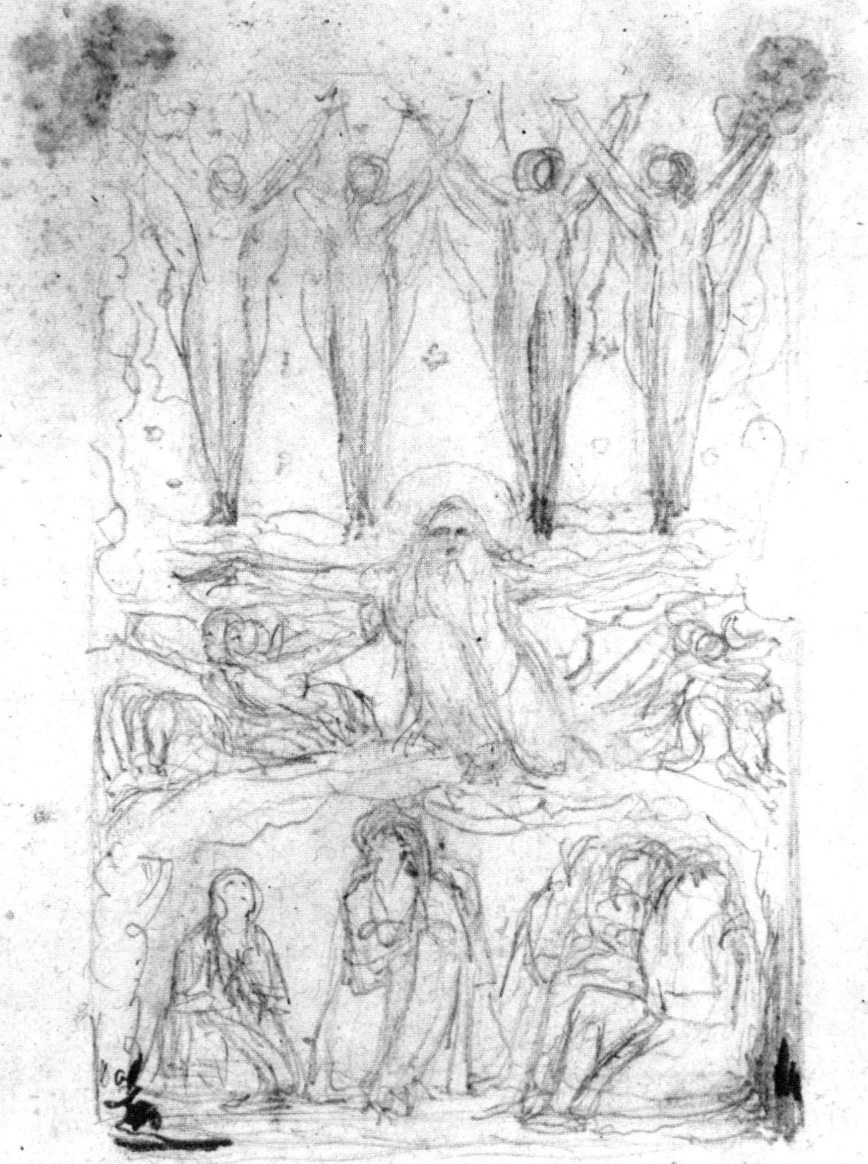

Done by

14A When the Morning Stars Sang Together ca. 1823
pencil and india ink
5 3/4 x 3 5/8 inches (146 x 92 mm)

inscribed *14*, top right. Signed *done by* followed by five symbols (not entirely a rebus), below right.

The Syndics of the Fitzwilliam Museum, Cambridge, England, PD.40-1950

reference: Bindman 1970, p. 48, no. 39(16)

According to Wicksteed (1971), the symbolical signature consists of: a straight line for immortality (or eternity); a hand; a capital "B" for Blake or a thumb; an eye; a circle for symmetry. The complete signature symbolizes the Poetic Genius as revealed through Blake's art. Lindberg (1973) modifies this interpretation, pointing out that the circle at the end is flanked by two spots, probably to represent the earth encircled by the sun and moon (or symmetry) as in the margin of the engraving. "B" for Blake is flanked by the hand and the upward-looking eye of the inspired artist and acts as intermediary between the infinite spiritual world, represented on the left, and the finite natural world, on the right. Butlin (1981) is not altogether convinced of this interpretation. "Done by me, with my hand, and my eye which sees eternity," might be a safer reading.

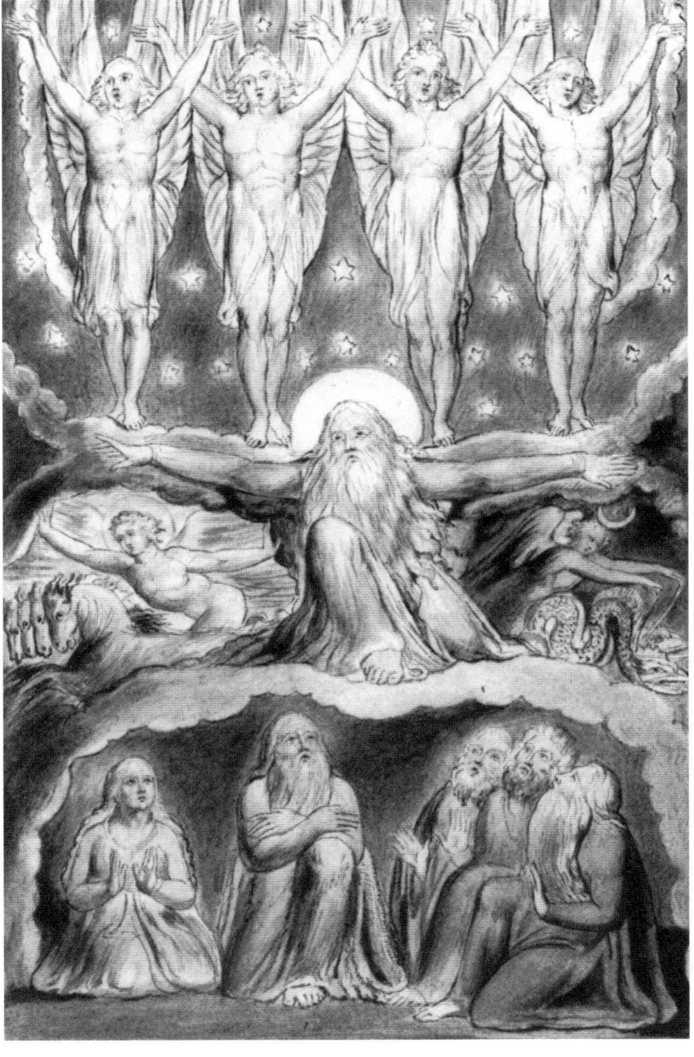

14B When the Morning Stars Sang Together ca. 1826
pencil and watercolor
5 3/4 x 3 3/4 inches (146 x 95 mm)

Yale Center for British Art, New Haven, Paul Mellon Collection, B.1992.8.7(15)

reference: Bindman 1987a, pl. 14c; 1987b, 1:16; 2: pl.14

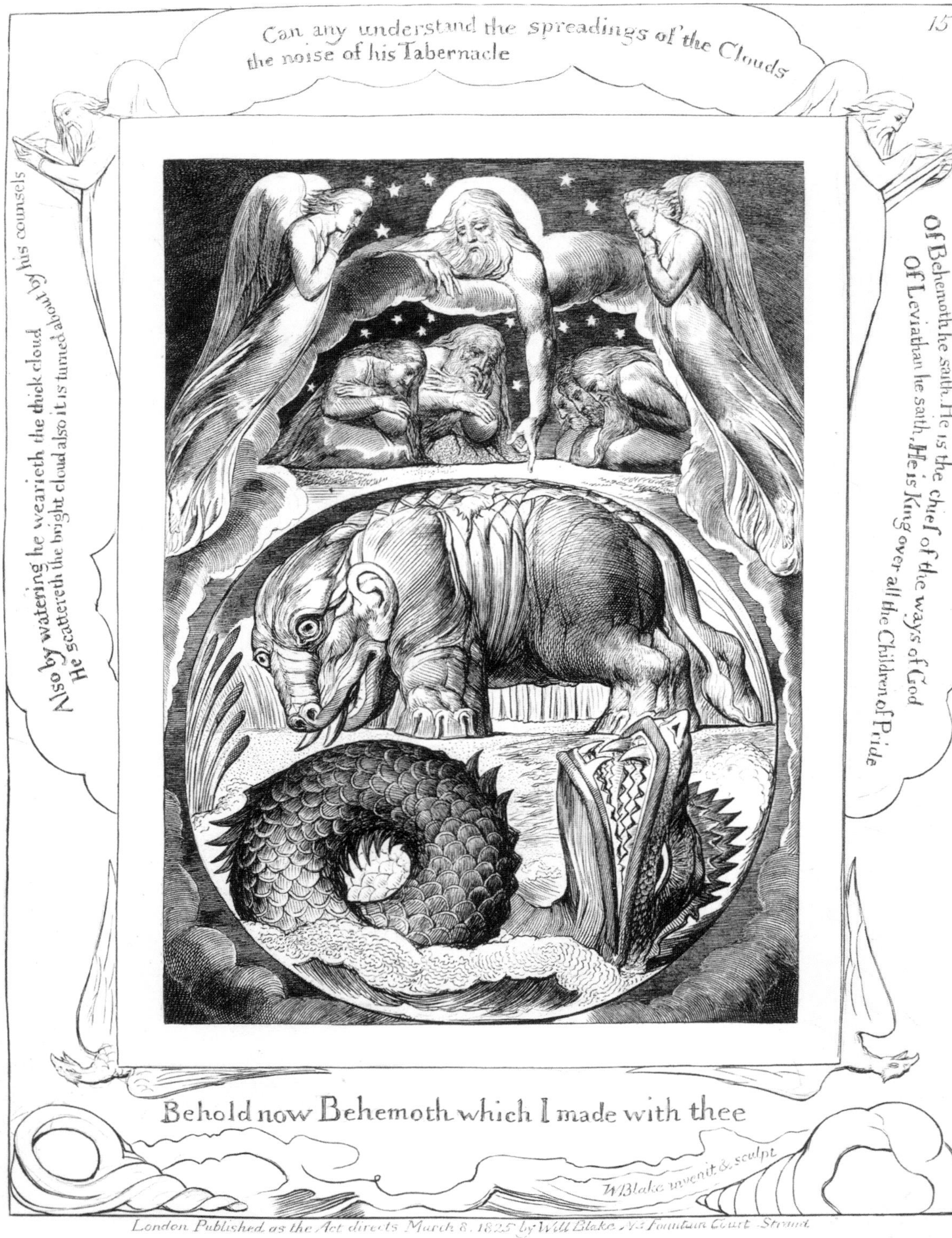

Can any understand the spreadings of the Clouds
the noise of his Tabernacle

Also by watering he wearieth the thick cloud
He scattereth the bright cloud also it is turned about by his counsels

Of Behemoth he saith. He is the chief of the ways of God
Of Leviathan he saith. He is King over all the Children of Pride

Behold now Behemoth which I made with thee

W Blake invenit & sculpt

London Published as the Act directs March 8. 1825 by Will Blake No 3 Fountain Court Strand

PLATE 15

Behemoth and Leviathan

ENGRAVING; DESIGN 7 3/4 X 5 7/8 INCHES (197 X 150 MM)

INSCRIBED ABOVE THE IMAGE: *Can any understand the spreadings of the Clouds / the noise of his Tabernacle* (JOB 36:29, PART OF ELIHU'S JUSTIFICATION OF GOD'S RIGHTEOUSNESS). IN LEFT MARGIN: *Also by watering he wearieth the thick cloud / He scattereth the* ["his" in the original] *bright cloud also it is turned about by his counsels* (JOB 37:11–12, ALSO PART OF ELIHU'S SPEECH). IN THE RIGHT MARGIN: *Of Behemoth he saith. He is the chief of the ways of God / Of Leviathan he saith. He is King over all the Children of Pride* (JOB 40:19 AND JOB 41:34). BELOW THE IMAGE: *Behold now Behemoth which I made with thee* (JOB 40:15). SIGNED ON PLATE, LOWER RIGHT, WITH PUBLISHER'S IMPRINT UNDERNEATH. WATERMARK: *J WATERMAN TURKEY MILL 1825.*

In the second of Job's visions of God's creation, God, flanked by angels, with Job and his companions on the flat earth underneath, points down to the globe of his creation. The monster Behemoth (a cross between a ferocious hippopotamus and Dürer's engraving of a rhinoceros) was created at the same time as humankind and dominates the land, while churning in the sea is the scaly monster Leviathan.

For Blake, both upper and lower visions are indicative of materialist forces. A scientific view of the earth as a globe for him was "mere Nature or Hell." Inspiration told him that the earth is flat and the sky domed; as he said to Crabb Robinson, "I do not believe that the world is round, I believe it is quite flat." But, according to Blake, at least Job was willing to acknowledge that God was capable of creating these two opposites that dominated the lands and the sea. He had, indeed, used images of both creatures before, particularly in his paintings for *The Spiritual Form of Pitt Guiding Behemoth* (1805) and *The Spiritual Form of Nelson Guiding Leviathan* (1805–1823). In this image they are interpreted as inhabitants of a materialistic hell, which God has revealed to Job, as part of his powers.

The top corners of the inner border support bearded angels; eagles spread their wings along the bottom corners. Underneath, waves break between seashells.

Virginia Museum of Fine Arts Purchase, The Arthur and Margaret Glasgow Fund, 73.80.16/22

REFERENCE: Bindman 1987a, pp. 82–83 (text); pl. 15

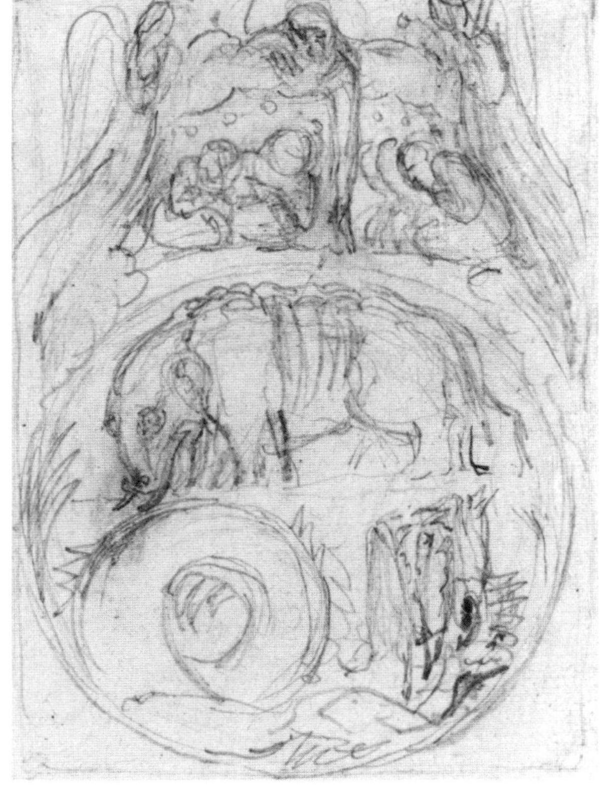

15A BEHEMOTH AND LEVIATHAN CA. 1823
PENCIL AND INDIA INK
5 5/8 X 3 7/8 INCHES (146 X 99 MM)
INSCRIBED *15*, top right
The Syndics of the Fitzwilliam Museum, Cambridge, England, PD.41-1950
REFERENCE: Bindman 1970, p. 48, no. 39(17)

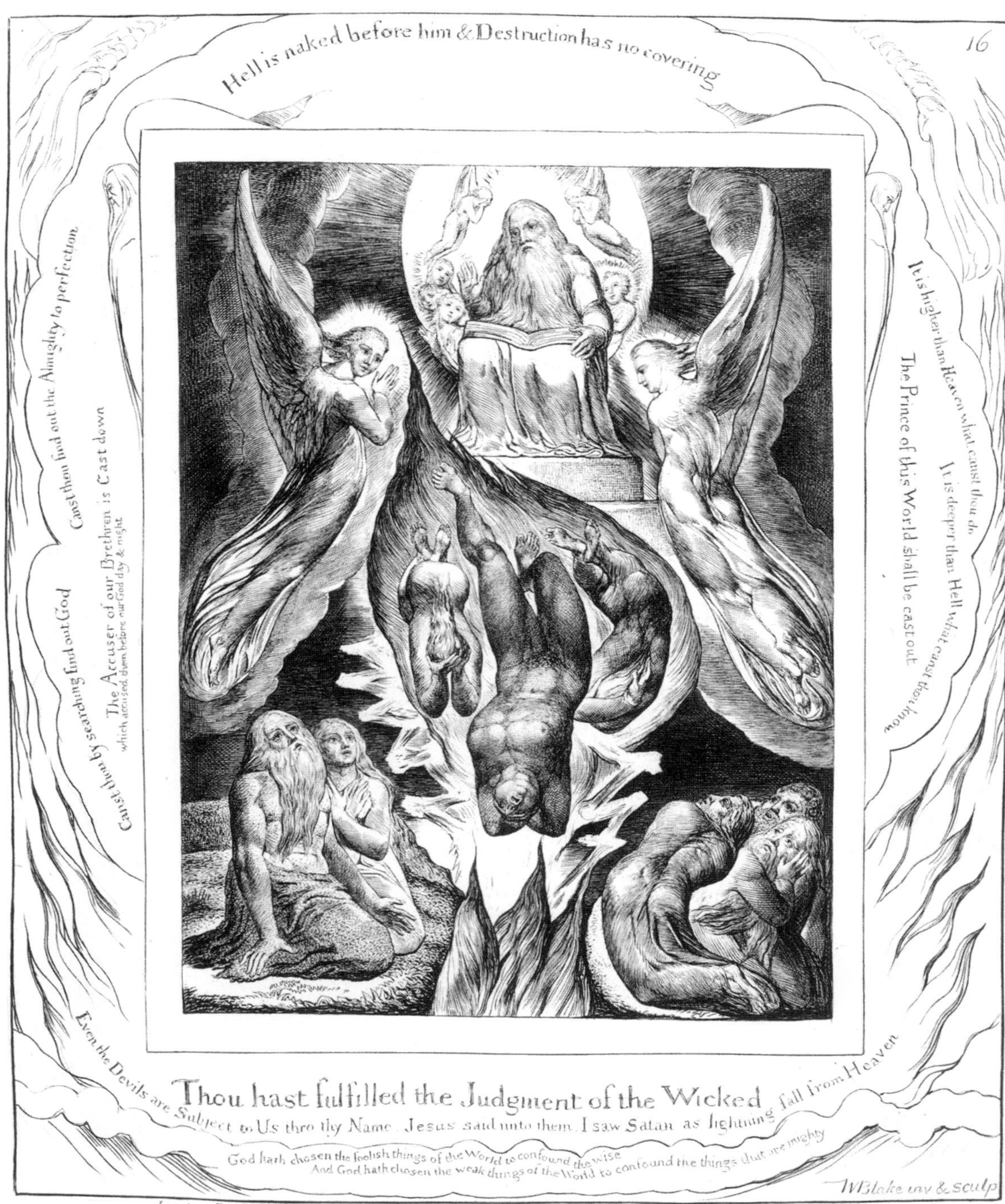
16
Hell is naked before him & Destruction has no covering
Canst thou by searching find out God
Canst thou find out the Almighty to perfection
The Accuser of our Brethren is Cast down
which accused them before our God day & night
It is higher than Heaven what canst thou do
It is deeper than Hell what canst thou know
The Prince of this World shall be cast out
Thou hast fulfilled the Judgment of the Wicked
Even the Devils are Subject to Us thro thy Name. Jesus said unto them. I saw Satan as lightning fall from Heaven
God hath chosen the foolish things of the World to confound the wise
And God hath chosen the weak things of the World to confound the things that are mighty
WBlake inv & sculp
London. Published as the Act directs March 8:1825 by William Blake No 3 Fountain Court Strand

PLATE 16

The Fall of Satan

ENGRAVING; DESIGN AREA 7 3/16 X 5 7/8 INCHES (182 X 149 MM)

INSCRIBED ABOVE THE IMAGE: *Hell is naked before him & Destruction has no covering* (JOB 26:6, PART OF JOB'S EARLIER ANSWER TO BILDAD). LEFT MARGIN: *Canst thou by searching find out God. / Canst thou find out the Almighty to perfection* (JOB 11:7, ZOPHAR'S QUESTIONS TO JOB) / *The Accuser of our Brethren is Cast down / which accused them before our God day & night* (REVELATION 12: 10). RIGHT MARGIN: *It is higher than Heaven what canst thou do / It is deeper than Hell what canst thou know* (JOB 11:8, ZOPHAR'S QUESTIONS TO JOB) / *The Prince of this World shall be cast out* (JOHN 12:31, PART OF JESUS' PROPHECIES ABOUT HIS CRUCIFIXION, AS HE ENTERED JERUSALEM). BELOW THE IMAGE: *Thou has fulfilled the Judgment of the Wicked* (JOB 36:17, PART OF ELIHU'S SPEECH TO JOB) / *Even the Devils are Subject to Us thro thy Name. Jesus said unto them. I saw Satan as lightning fall from Heaven* (LUKE 10:17-18, THE DISCIPLES' REPORT OF THEIR SUCCESS AND JESUS' REPLY TO THEM) / *God hath chosen the foolish things of the World to confound the wise / And God hath chosen the weak things of the World to confound the things that are mighty* (1 CORINTHIANS 1:27, PART OF PAUL'S EPISTLE TO THE CORINTHIANS). SIGNED ON PLATE, LOWER RIGHT, WITH PUBLISHER'S IMPRINT UNDERNEATH.

God as Christ reveals to Job and his wife the defeat of Satan at the Last Judgment (which is not described in the *Book of Job* but in the New Testament). Satan, accompanied by a man and woman, are cast down into a fiery pit. Job's friends do not seem able to comprehend what is happening. The weeping angels in God's halo are not, apparently, weeping at Satan's fate but, as Lindberg (1973) suggests, quoting from the Vulgate version of the Bible, they are weeping "their false pity out of themselves, and are cleansed."

Blake was concerned with other visions of the Last Judgment in his lost tempera painting, shown at his exhibition of 1809, and in his writings *The Song of Los, The Four Zoas, Milton,* and *Jerusalem.* He was much impressed by Michelangelo's fresco in the Sistine Chapel, although he only knew it from engravings. Blake thought that "whenever any individual Rejects Error and Embraces Truth, a Last Judgment passes upon that Individual" (from his description of his lost tempera painting, *The Last Judgment*).

Virginia Museum of Fine Arts Purchase, The Arthur and Margaret Glasgow Fund, 73.80.17/22

REFERENCE: Bindman 1987a, pp. 83–85 (text); pl. 16

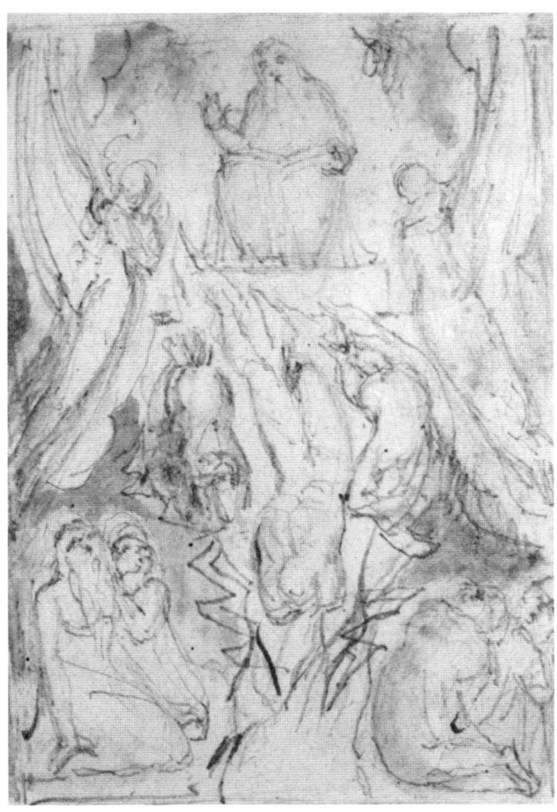

16A THE FALL OF SATAN CA. 1823
PENCIL AND WATERCOLOR
5 1/4 X 3 5/8 INCHES (133 X 92 MM)

INSCRIBED *16*, top right

The Syndics of the Fitzwilliam Museum, Cambridge, England, PD.42-1950

REFERENCE: Bindman 1970, p. 48, no. 39(18)

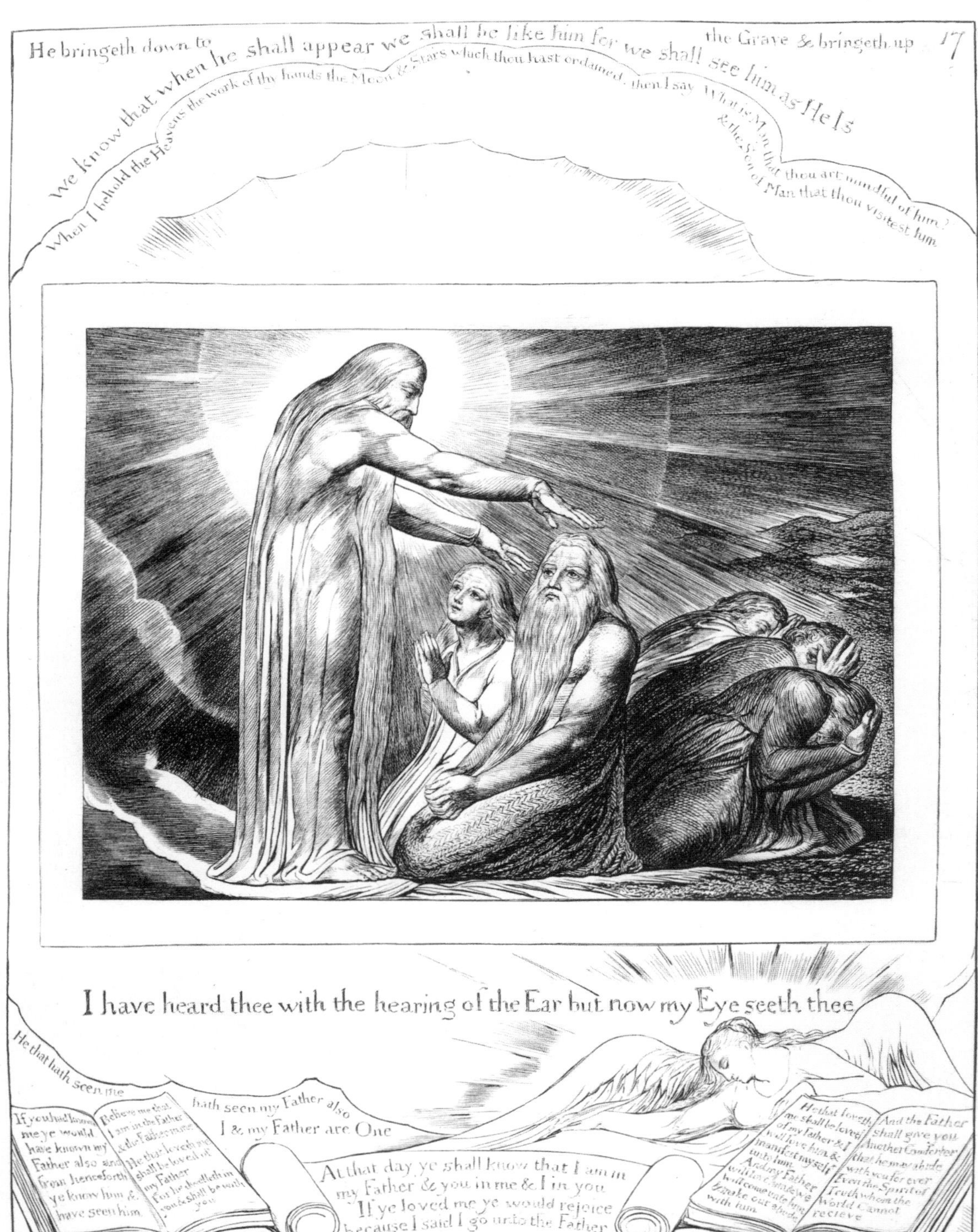

London Published as the Act directs March 8 1825 by William Blake N 3 Fountain Court Strand

PLATE 17

The Vision of Christ

ENGRAVING; DESIGN 7 3/4 X 5 13/16 INCHES (196 X 148 MM)

INSCRIBED ABOVE THE IMAGE: *He bringeth down to / the Grave & bringeth up* (1 SAMUEL 2:6, PART OF HANNAH'S PRAYER IN PRAISE OF GOD) / *We know that when he shall appear we shall be like him for we shall see him as He Is* (1 JOHN 3:2) / *When I behold the Heavens the work of thy hands the Moon & Stars which thou hast ordained. then I say What is Man that thou art mindful of him? / & the Son of Man that thou visitest him* (PSALMS 8:3-4, WITH SOME CHANGES). BELOW THE IMAGE: *I have heard thee with the hearing of the Ear but now my Eye seeth thee* (JOB 42:5, JOB'S RECONCILIATION WITH GOD) / *He that hath seen me / hath seen my Father also* (JOHN 14:9, JESUS' WORDS AT THE LAST SUPPER) / *I & my Father are One* (JOHN 10:30); INSCRIBED ON BOOKS AND SCROLLS: *If you had known / me ye would / have known my / Father also and / from henceforth / ye know him & / have seen him / Believe me that / I am in the Father / & the Father in me / He that loveth me / shall be loved of / my Father / For he dwelleth in / you and shall be with / you; At that day ye shall know that I am in / my Father & you in me & I in you / If ye loved me ye would rejoice / because I said I go unto the Father; He that loveth / me shall be loved / of my Father & I / will love him & / manifest myself / unto him / And my Father / will love him & we / will come unto him / & make our abode / with him / And the Father / shall give you / Another Comforter / that he may abide / with you for ever / Even the Spirit of / Truth whom the / World Cannot / recieve* [SIC] (JOHN 14, CHRIST'S WORDS TO THE DISCIPLES, MUCH REARRANGED). SIGNED ON PLATE ALONG BOTTOM EDGE ON EITHER SIDE OF THE SCROLL, WITH PUBLISHER'S IMPRINT UNDERNEATH.

In this image, for which he has quoted only one line from Job, Blake has placed the blessing of Job and his wife by God (as Christ) before Job's Prayer in plate 18, whereas the biblical account puts God's blessing toward the end of the story (42:12). Job's friends crouch at the right unable to see the vision of the unity of the Father and the Son with mankind, which early Church fathers saw as the point of the Job story. Lindberg (1973) identified the female angel holding the pen in the lower margin as St. John's muse. The figure of God may be based, as Lindberg suggested, on the figure of St. Paul in Raphael's cartoon of *St. Paul Preaching at Athens*, then as now in the Royal Collection, but known from engravings.

Virginia Museum of Fine Arts Purchase, The Arthur and Margaret Glasgow Fund, 73.80.18/22

REFERENCE: Bindman 1987a, pp. 85–87 (text); pl. 17

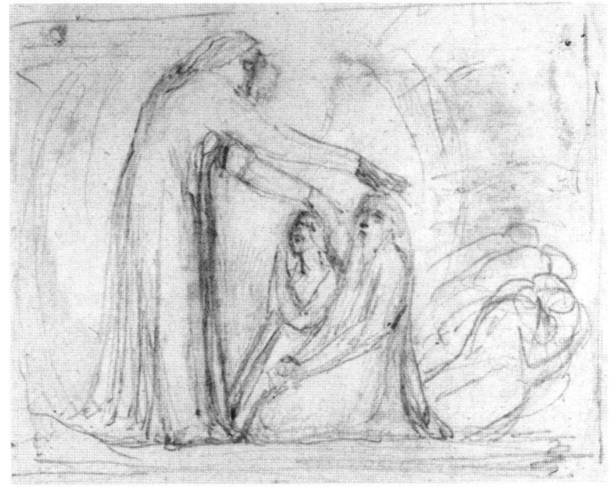

17A THE VISION OF CHRIST CA. 1823
PENCIL AND WATERCOLOR
3 3/4 X 4 11/16 INCHES

INSCRIBED *10*, top right

The Syndics of the Fitzwilliam Museum, Cambridge, England, PD.43-1950

REFERENCE: Bindman 1970, p. 48, no. 39(19)

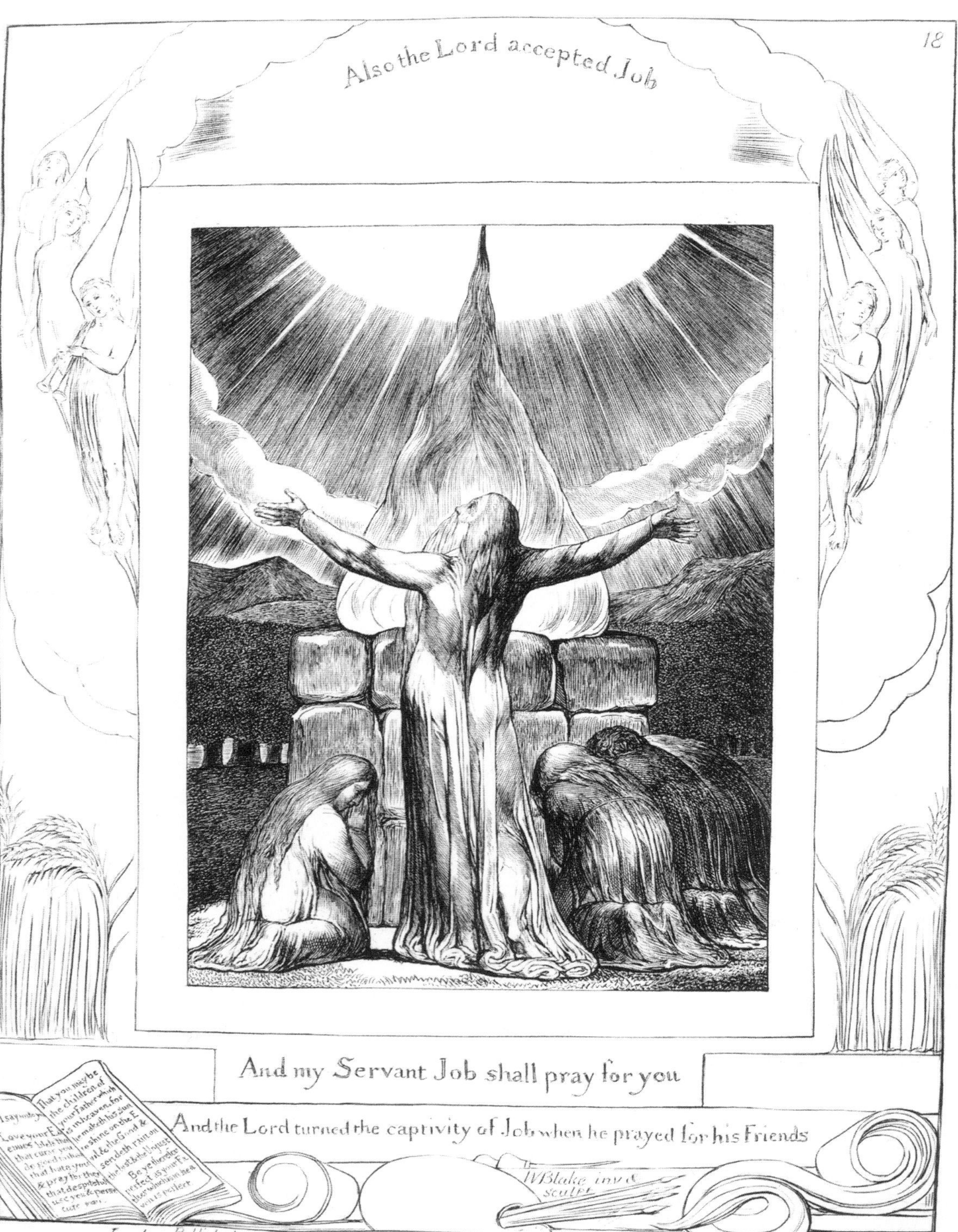
18
Also the Lord accepted Job
And my Servant Job shall pray for you
And the Lord turned the captivity of Job when he prayed for his Friends
Love your E
& pray for them
that despitefull
use you & perse
cute you.
That you may be
the children of
your Father which
is in heaven. for
he maketh his Sun
to shine on the E
vil & the Good &
sendeth rain on
the Just & the Unjust
Be ye therefore
perfect as your Fa
ther which in hea
ven is perfect
W Blake inv &
sculpt
London Published as the Act directs March 8. 1825 by Will Blake No 3 Fountain Court Strand

PLATE 18

Job's Sacrifice

ENGRAVING; DESIGN 7 1/2 X 5 13/16 INCHES (191 X 147 MM)

INSCRIBED ABOVE THE IMAGE: *Also the Lord accepted Job* (JOB 42:9); BELOW THE IMAGE: *And my Servant Job shall pray for you* (JOB 42:8) / *And the Lord turned the captivity of Job when he prayed for his Friends* (JOB 42: 10). INSCRIBED ON BOOK LOWER LEFT: *I say unto you / Love your En/emies bless them / that curse you / do good to those / that hate you / & pray for they / that despite-full[y] / use you & perse / cute you / That you may be / the children of / your Father which / is in heaven. for / he maketh his Sun / to shine on the E / vil & the Good & / sendeth rain on / the Just & the Unjust / Be ye therefore / perfect as your Fa / ther which is in hea / ven is perfect* (MATTHEW 5:44–45; 48, PART OF CHRIST'S SERMON ON THE MOUNT). SIGNED ON PLATE, LOWER CENTER, WITH PUBLISHER'S IMPRINT UNDERNEATH.

In this image, as the quotations from the Sermon on the Mount emphasize, Job prays for his friends, who are now forgiven. In the *Book of Job*, God is angry with the friends for not obeying Him as Job did. From Job's altar the flame reaches the spiritual sun, not the natural sun, for the scene seems to be set at dawn. As Blake remarked to Crabb Robinson: "*You* never saw the spiritual sun. I have. I saw him on Primrose Hill" (Morley 1938). As a result of suffering, Job (and Blake, the mystic) have affected a union with God the Father, Jesus, and the Holy Ghost through a forgiveness of sins. The images at the bottom of a palette with brushes and two engraver's tools (burins), and the angels making music above, unite the arts and the imagination with Christ. As Blake wrote in *The Lacoön,* "Jesus & his Apostles & Disciples were all Artists."

Virginia Museum of Fine Arts Purchase, The Arthur and Margaret Glasgow Fund, 73.80.19/22

REFERENCE: Bindman 1987a, pp. 87–89 (text); pl. 18

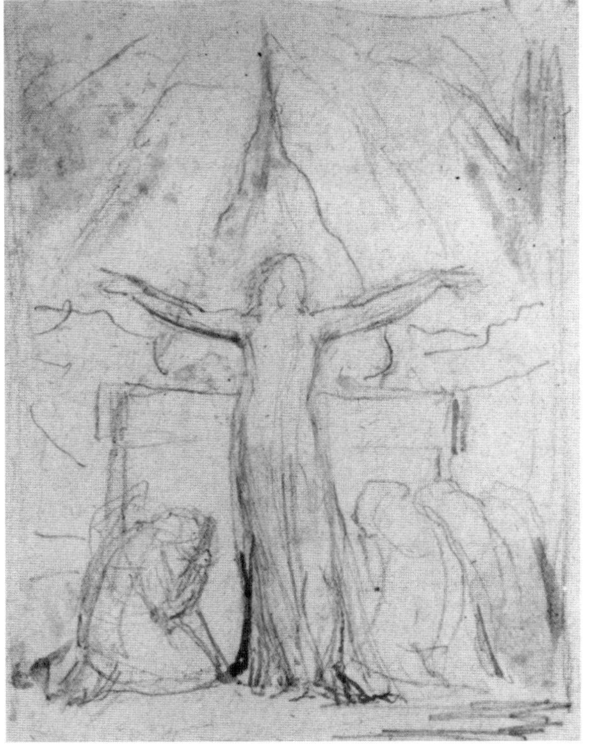

18A JOB'S SACRIFICE CA. 1823
PENCIL AND INK WASH
4 7/8 X 3 5/8 INCHES (124 X 92 MM)

INSCRIBED *18*, top right

The verso has a faint pencil sketch for *Job and His Daughters*, plate 20.

The Syndics of the Fitzwilliam Museum, Cambridge, England, PD.44-1950

REFERENCE: Bindman 1970, p. 48, no. 39(20)

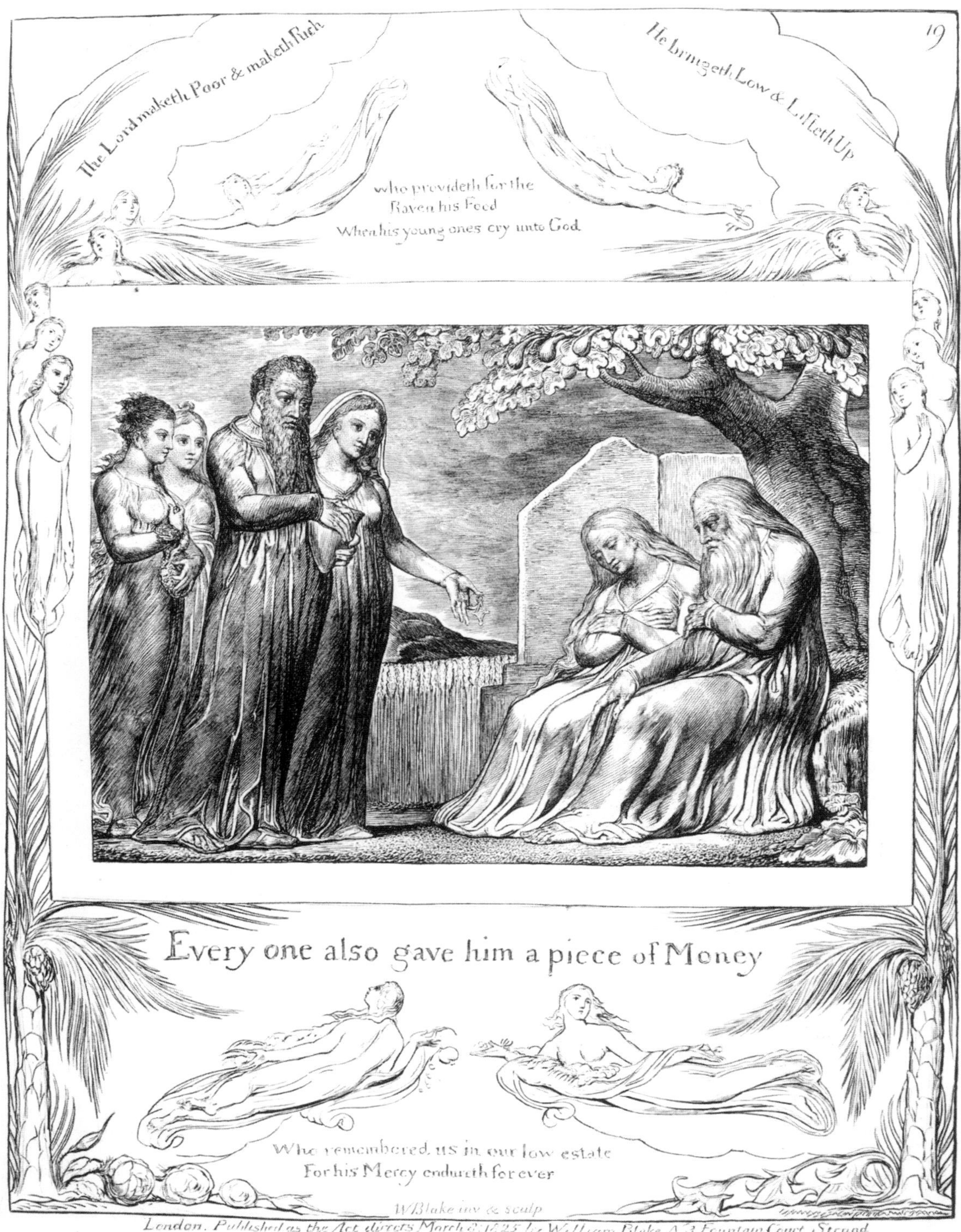
19
The Lord maketh Poor & maketh Rich
He bringeth Low & Lifteth Up
who provideth for the
Raven his Food
When his young ones cry unto God
Every one also gave him a piece of Money
Who remembered us in our low estate
For his Mercy endureth for ever
W Blake inv & sculp
London. Published as the Act directs March 8: 1825 by William Blake No 3 Fountain Court Strand

PLATE 19

Every Man Also Gave Him a Piece of Money

ENGRAVING; DESIGN 7 9/16 X 5 7/8 INCHES (192 X 148 MM)

INSCRIBED ABOVE THE IMAGE, ON THE RIGHT: *The Lord maketh Poor & maketh Rich;* ON THE LEFT, *He bringeth Low and Lifteth Up* (1 SAMUEL 2:7, ANOTHER PART OF HANNAH'S PRAYER); AND IN THE MIDDLE, *who provideth for the / Raven his Food / When his young ones cry unto God* (JOB 38:41, PART OF GOD'S ANSWER TO JOB, OUT OF THE WHIRLWIND). BELOW THE IMAGE: *Every one also gave him a piece of Money* (JOB 42:11, ONE OF THE REWARDS OF JOB'S RECONCILIATION WITH GOD) / *Who remembered us in our low estate / For his Mercy endureth for ever* (PSALMS 136:23). SIGNED ON PLATE, BOTTOM CENTER, WITH PUBLISHER'S IMPRINT UNDERNEATH.

Although Job's house is in ruins, and he and his wife are seated at the right as they were in plate 4, he is now receiving gifts instead of tidings of misfortune. Everywhere in the design are signs of abundance: in the background of the main image is a field full of ripe wheat; the margins show palm trees bearing fruit; and female figures sow seeds (above), and bear cornucopias of fruit and flowers (below). The image may also bear an autobiographical reference to Blake's debt to his patrons—Butts or Linnell—for a new prosperity. As Wicksteed (1971) pointed out, the gifts are from God, and "the righteous shall flourish like a palm tree" (PSALMS 92:12).

Virginia Museum of Fine Arts Purchase, The Arthur and Margaret Glasgow Fund, 73.80.20/22

REFERENCE: Bindman 1987a, pp. 89–91 (text); pl. 19

19B [AT RIGHT] STUDY FOR ALTERNATIVE COMPOSITION FOR PLATE 19 CA. 1823
EVERY MAN ALSO GAVE HIM A PIECE OF MONEY
PENCIL AND WATERCOLOR
5 3/8 X 4 1/8 INCHES (133 X 115 MM)

The design from the Linnell set (SEE P. 14), originally traced by John Linnell, with additions by Blake, enlarged the horizontal design of the Butts set by adding another figure at the left. Two further designs (Butlin nos. 553 and 554) experimented with the rejected vertical design of the Fitzwilliam drawing. This vertical design was not followed in the engraving, perhaps because the vision of God is so similar to that in plate 20.

The Syndics of the Fitzwilliam Museum, Cambridge, England, PD.46-1950

REFERENCE: Bindman 1970, p. 49, no. 39(21) recto

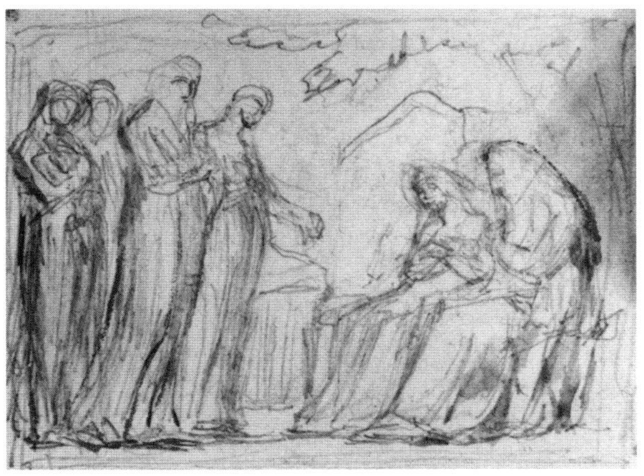

19A EVERY MAN ALSO GAVE HIM A PIECE OF MONEY
CA. 1823
PENCIL, INDIA INK AND GREY WASH
3 1/4 X 4 3/8 INCHES (83 X 111 MM)
INSCRIBED *19*, top right

This design was the one adapted for the finished engraving.

The Syndics of the Fitzwilliam Museum, Cambridge, England, PD.45-1950

REFERENCE: Bindman 1970, p. 49, no. 39(23) recto

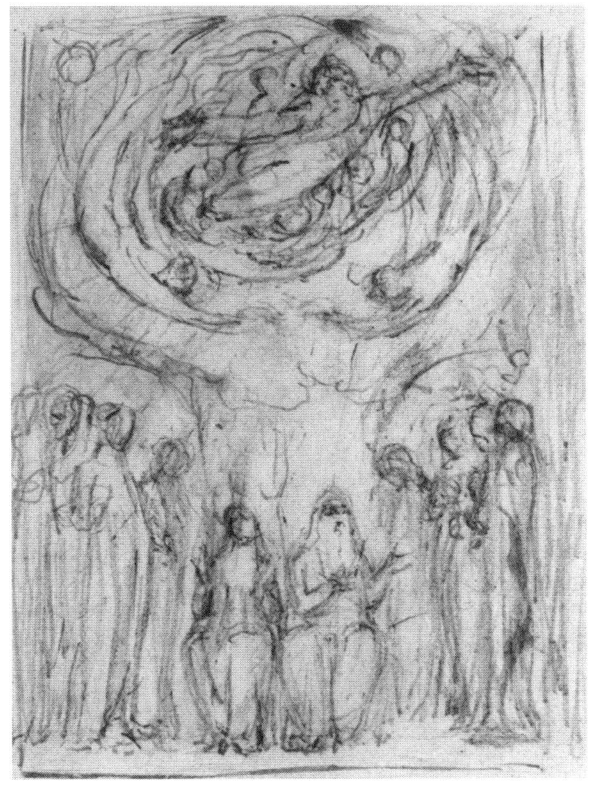

How precious are thy thoughts
unto me O God
how great is the sum of them

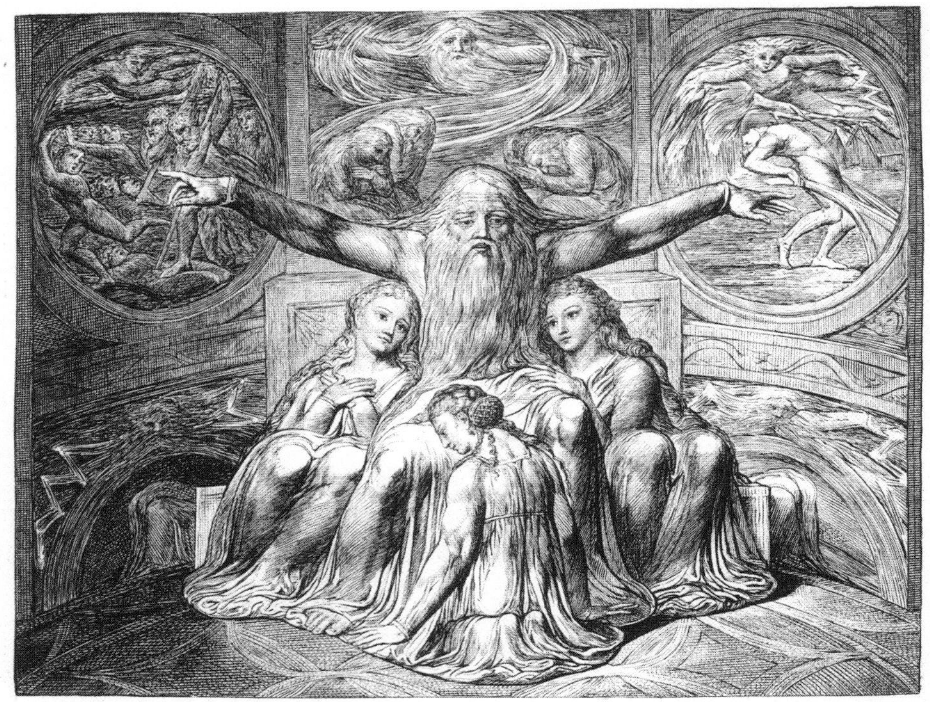

There were not found Women fair as the Daughters of Job
in all the Land & their Father gave them Inheritance
among their Brethren

If I ascend up into Heaven thou art there
If I make my bed in Hell behold Thou
art there

W Blake invent & sc

London. Published as the Act directs March 8: 1825 by William Blake No 3 Fountain Court Strand

PLATE 20

Job and His Daughters

ENGRAVING, DESIGN 7 3/4 X 5 7/8 INCHES (197 X 150 MM)

INSCRIBED ABOVE THE IMAGE: *How precious are thy thoughts / unto me O God / how great is the sum of them* (PSALMS 139:17); BELOW THE IMAGE: *There were not found Women fair as the Daughters of Job / in all the Land & their Father gave them Inheritance / among their Brethren* (JOB 42:15) / *If I ascend up into Heaven thou art there / If I make my bed in Hell behold Thou / art there* (PSALMS 139:8). SIGNED ON PLATE, AT LOWER RIGHT MARGIN, WITH PUBLISHER'S IMPRINT UNDERNEATH.

In this image, which differs from the Pierpont Morgan watercolor (SEE NO. 20A) in which the scene is set outdoors, Job is recounting to his daughters his previous misfortunes. These three daughters, Jemima, Kezia, and Kerenhappuch, were born along with seven sons after Job had been restored to prosperity, his first family apparently having been killed. In the Pierpont Morgan watercolor they are shown taking down their father's words. The round paintings, or tondos, on the side walls, to which Job is pointing, refer to the earlier events of Job's life. At the left Satan watches as the Sabeans kill his sons, while at the right Satan kills his ploughman. In the center God speaks to Job out of the whirlwind. Lower down are semicircular images of Job's wife.

As Lindberg (1973) has shown, the scene does not occur in the *Book of Job* but is taken from the Apocryphal *Testament of Job*, as are a number of other details in Blake's *Illustrations*, for example: Job sharing his last loaf with a beggar (plate 5), Satan masquerading as God (plate 11), and Job as a holy musician and singer of celestial songs (see plate 21). The lyre and the lute in the margin seem to look forward to the final scene (plate 21). The margins are filled with vine leaves that may symbolize either Job's love for his family, hence the loving angels above, or the relationship between Christ and the Church.

Virginia Museum of Fine Arts Purchase, The Arthur and Margaret Glasgow Fund, 73.80.21/22

REFERENCE: Bindman 1987a, pp. 91–93 (text); pl. 20

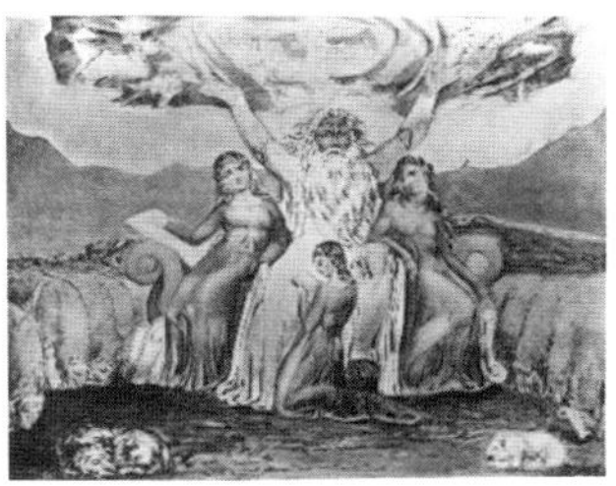

20A JOB AND HIS DAUGHTERS CA. 1804–7
(COLOR PLATE VI)
PEN AND WATERCOLOR
8 11/16 X 10 7/8 INCHES (220 X 276 MM)

Differs from plate 20 in that it is set out-of-doors. Probably nearer in date to the engravings than the other watercolors in the Butts set, and with the intervention of others, possibly Mrs. Blake. (SEE INTRODUCTION, P. 16.)

The Pierpont Morgan Library, New York, III, 45, PLATE 20

REFERENCE: Butlin 1981, p. 417, no. 550.20, pl. 716

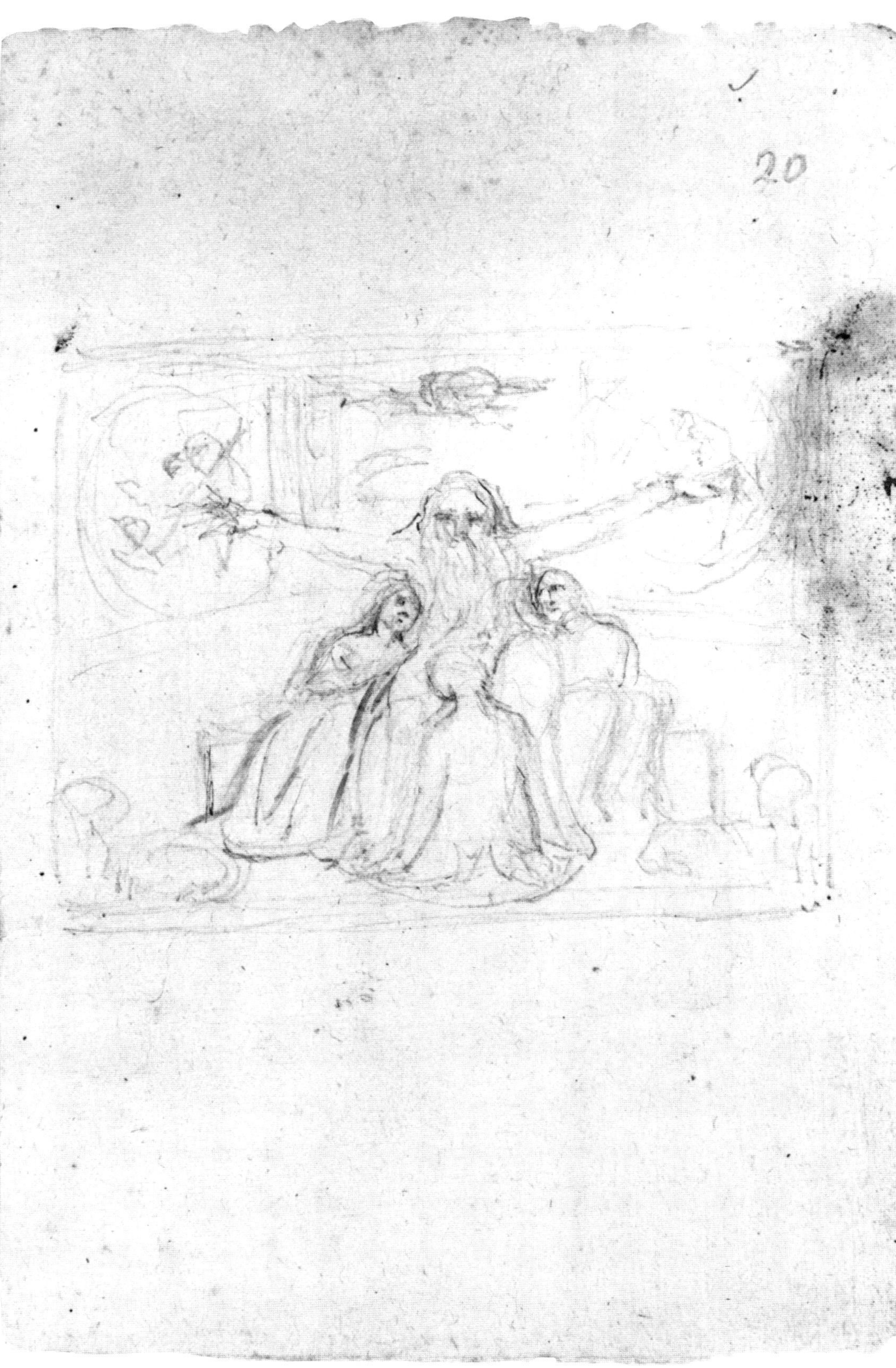

20B JOB AND HIS DAUGHTERS CA. 1823
PEN AND PENCIL
3 7/8 X 4 7/8 INCHES (99 X 124 MM)

INSCRIBED *20,* top right

The Syndics of the Fitzwilliam Museum, Cambridge, England, PD.47-1950

The engraving, plate 20, is set indoors and omits the sheep in the foreground. The composition reverts to the Butts tempera of about 1799–1800, also set out-of-doors, which has suggestions of the roundels in the background. A further faint pencil sketch for this design is on the verso of *Job's Sacrifice* (NO. 18A).

REFERENCE: Bindman 1970, p. 49, no. 39(24)

20C JOB AND HIS DAUGHTERS CA. 1826
PENCIL AND WATERCOLOR
3 3/4 X 4 3/4 INCHES (95 X 121 MM)

Yale Center for British Art, New Haven, Paul Mellon Collection, B. 1992.8.7(21)

REFERENCE: Bindman 1987a, pl. 20c; 1987b, 1:18–19; 2:pl. 20

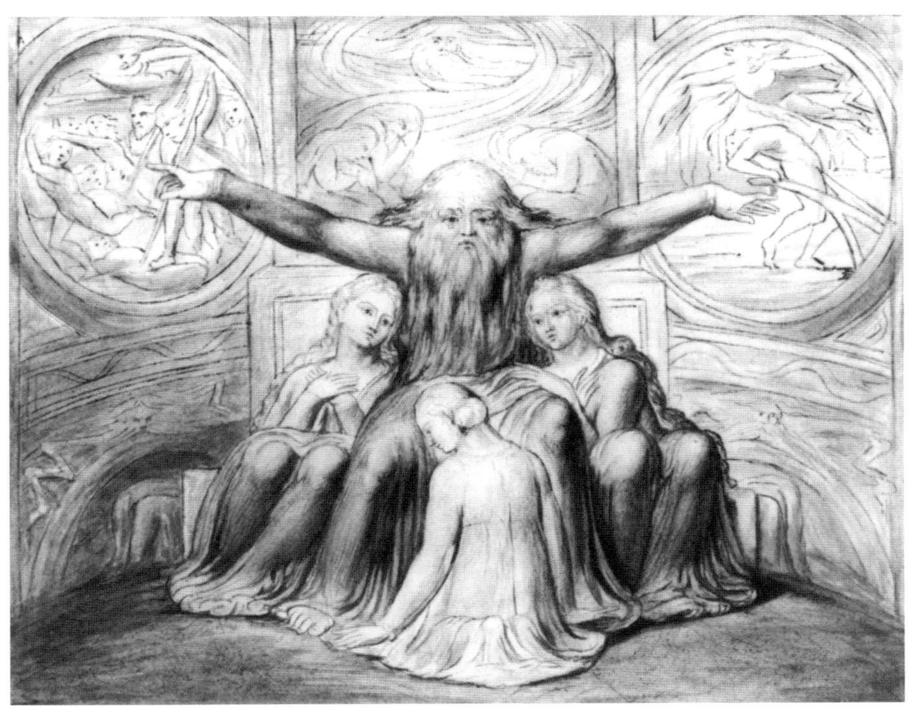

21

Great & Marvellous are thy Works
Lord God Almighty

Just & True are thy Ways
O thou King of Saints

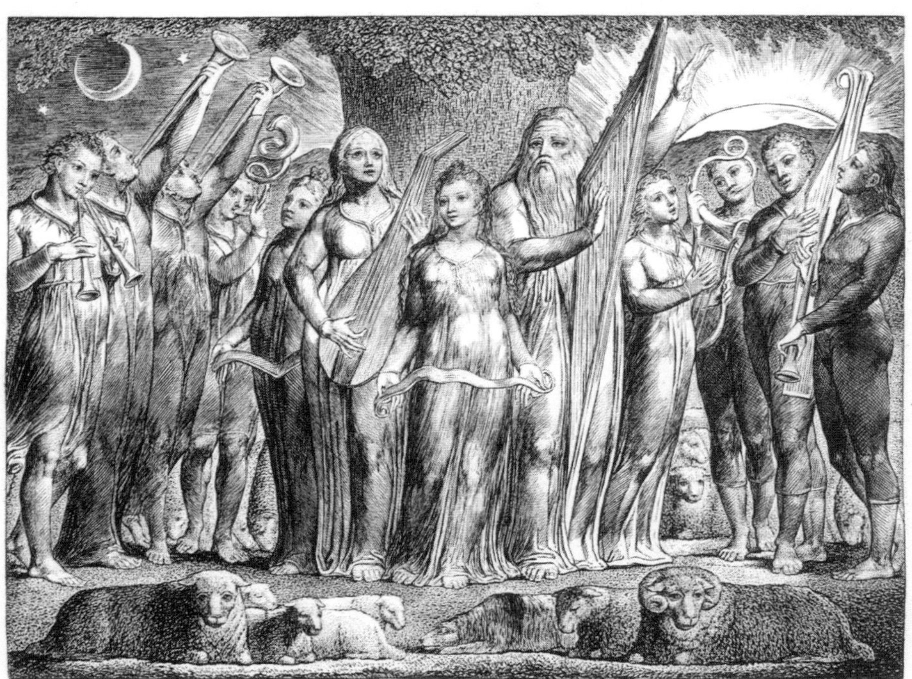

So the Lord bleſsed the latter end of Job
more than the beginning

After this Job lived
an hundred & forty years
& saw his Sons & his
Sons Sons

even four Generations
So Job died
being old
& full of days

In burnt Offerings for Sin
thou hast had no Pleasure

W Blake inv & sculp

London Published as the Act directs March 8: 1825 by William Blake Fountain Court Strand

PLATE 21

Job and His Family Restored to Prosperity

ENGRAVING; DESIGN 7 11/16 X 5 7/8 INCHES (195 X 145 MM)

INSCRIBED ABOVE THE IMAGE: *Great & Marvellous are thy Works / Lord God Almighty / Just & True are thy Ways / O thou King of Saints* (REVELATION 15:3, THE SONGS OF MOSES AND THE SONG OF THE LAMB); BELOW THE IMAGE: *So the Lord blessed the latter end of Job / more than the beginning* (JOB 42:12) / *After this Job lived / an hundred & forty years / & saw his Sons & his / Sons Sons / even four Generations / So Job died / being old / & full of days* (JOB 42:16–17). ON ALTAR, LOWER CENTER: *In burnt Offerings for Sin / thou hast had no Pleasure* (EPISTLE TO THE HEBREWS 10:6). SIGNED ON PLATE LOWER RIGHT, WITH PUBLISHER'S IMPRINT UNDERNEATH.

21A JOB AND HIS FAMILY RESTORED TO PROSPERITY CA. 1823
PENCIL AND PEN
3 11/16 X 4 3/4 INCHES (94 X 120 MM)
INSCRIBED *21*, top right
The Syndics of the Fitzwilliam Museum, Cambridge, England, PD.48-1950
REFERENCE: Bindman 1970, p. 49, no. 39(22)

This is the spiritual counterpart of the first plate, which was inscribed *The Letter Killeth—the Spirit giveth Life*, with the sun now rising at the right and the new moon at the left. Job and his new generation of sons and daughters praise God with music, singing the song of Moses and the Lamb (see quotations from *Revelation*). In Blake's view Moses prefigured Christ, emphasized by the lamb and ox in the lower right- and left-hand corners, which often stood for Christ and Moses respectively (also seen in the first plate).

Music was a reflection of God's music, and Job and his family now reveal their joyful relationship with God by taking down the instruments that were hanging unused in a tree in plate 1. The quotation from Hebrews now emphasizes that their previous sacrifices to God brought no result. The figure of Job is close to that of the Ancient Bard in *The Voice of the Ancient Bard*, in Blake's *Songs of Experience*, 1794 (plate 54).

Virginia Museum of Fine Arts Purchase, The Arthur and Margaret Glasgow Fund, 73.80.22/22
REFERENCE: Bindman 1987a, pp. 93–95 (text); pl. 21

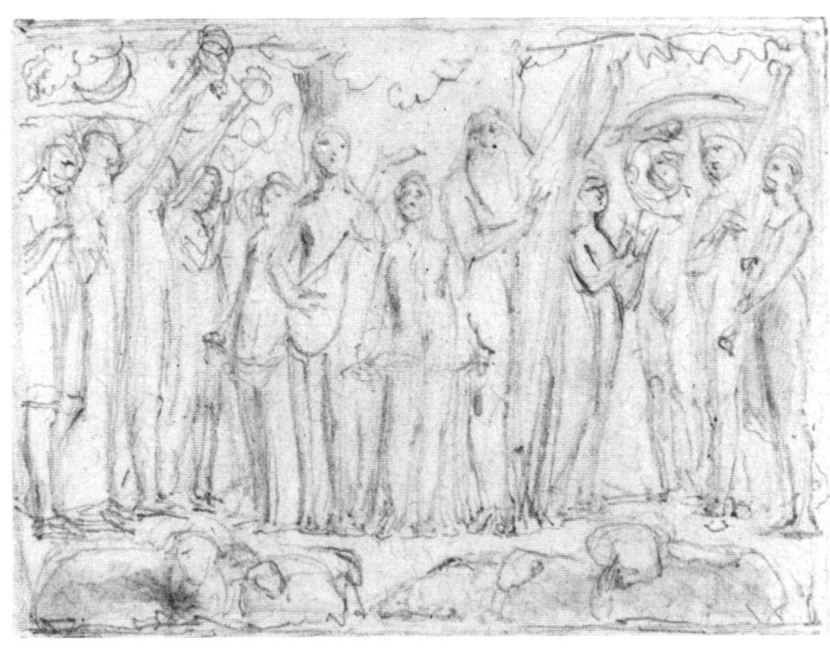

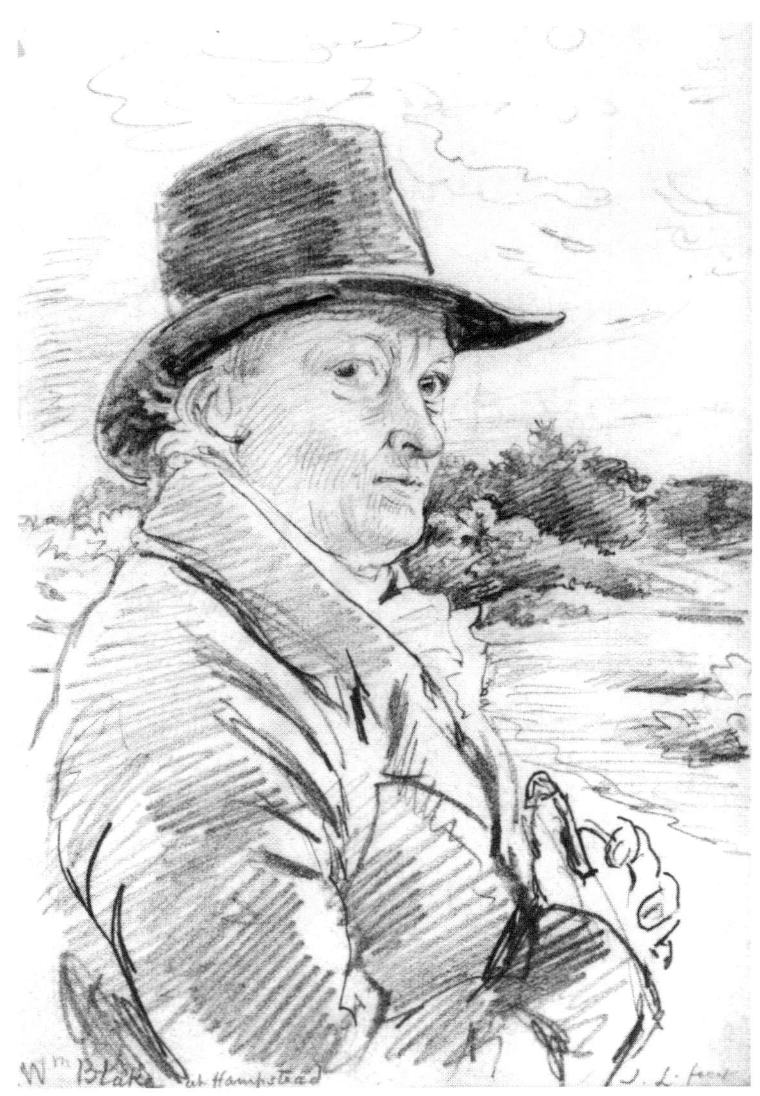

William Blake at Hampstead, circa 1825, by John Linnell (1792–1882), pencil on paper, 7 x 4 3/8 inches (177 x 112 MM). Linnell drew this portrait when Blake was finishing his work on the *Illustrations of the Book of Job*. Reproduced by permission of the Syndics of the Fitzwilliam Museum, Cambridge, England.

Afterword

The Book of Job Designs

from Butts Series to Final Engravings

DAVID BINDMAN
The Durning Lawrence Professor of Art History,
University College, University of London

Until recently it was usually assumed that the *Book of Job* illustrations were entirely a product of Blake's final years and that they were conceived and finally completed within a period of five to six years, from about 1820 to 1825. This assumption rested on the belief, which goes back to Blake's first biographer, Alexander Gilchrist,[1] that the first series of watercolor drawings (Pierpont Morgan Library), made for Blake's patron Thomas Butts, only just preceded the "Linnell set" (commissioned by Blake's friend, the artist John Linnell), which was partly traced from the earlier series in 1821. Though no new documentary evidence has emerged it is now clear from recent studies of the development of Blake's style that the Butts set was in fact made many years earlier, perhaps as early as 1804 and certainly no later than 1810.[2] The engravings of 1825–6 therefore can no longer be seen as the product of a single period in Blake's working life, but rather as the unforeseen result of the original series of watercolor drawings, which, over ten years after their completion, were given a new lease of life by the intervention of John Linnell. It follows that the Job designs must be seen as something more than a serene and autumnal expression of the artist's "old age style," for the essentials of Blake's interpretation of the biblical story of Job were well established by the end of the first decade of the century. The initial conception belongs not to the period of relative relaxation after the completion of *Jerusalem* in the early 1820s but to that seminal period when his prophecies *Milton* and *Jerusalem* were first in the process of formation, that is in the years after his return from Felpham in September 1803.

The first series made for Butts now consists of twenty-one watercolor drawings which correspond closely in their individual subjects to the final engravings (which have in addition a title page). Two of the designs, however, for numbers 17 and 20, are in a different style and were almost certainly added later, after the completion of the Linnell set in 1821.[3] The Butts set then probably consisted initially of nineteen designs, though it is not impossible that the two later designs replaced earlier versions with which Blake had become dissatisfied. It would be unwise to assume that the nineteen watercolor designs were designed and executed within a short space of time, but by applying Butlin's criteria for dating Blake's drawings we can place them firmly within the years around 1805.[4] They are more linear than the biblical watercolors, which can be dated on documentary evidence to 1800–3, but they lack the absolute linear clarity of the 1808 watercolors for *Paradise Lost* (Boston Museum of Fine Arts and elsewhere; Butlin nos. 536.1–12).[5] The extreme compositional symmetry which can be observed, especially in the first Butts drawing, is characteristic of Blake's work of around 1805, and the iconography of this first design, especially the instruments hanging on the tree, is close enough to a watercolor dated 1806 (*Waters of Babylon,* Butlin no. 466) to suggest a roughly comparable date. Similarities in drawing may also be observed with the 1807 *Paradise Lost* series (Huntington Library; Butlin no. 529), so it would seem safe to date the Butts series within the years 1804–7.

By the end of 1804 Blake was working on three major prophecies: *Vala or the Four Zoas* (British Library), begun in 1797, which he continued to revise extensively, abandoning it probably before 1807, and *Jerusalem* and *Milton,* which made rapid progress in the years 1804–7, though neither was printed until much later.[6] The problems of dating the last phase of revisions of *Vala or the Four Zoas* are complex, but it is generally agreed that the change in Blake's ideas in the years after 1800, when he went to Felpham, was fundamental enough to pull apart the structure he had erected before he left.[7] This mental change is expressed in a sense of spiritual renewal which begins to appear in his letters from 1802. On November 22 he writes, "I am again Emerged into the light of Day; I still & shall to Eternity Embrace Christianity and Adore him who is the Express image of God . . . Nothing can withstand the fury of my Course among the Stars of God & in the Abysses of the Accuser."[8] In a letter written that same day he adumbrates for the first time the idea of a Fourfold Vision. Blake had, of course, always been a Christian, but in this and subsequent letters he lays great emphasis on Jesus' role in the redemption of man. In a letter of April 25, 1803, he refers to "the Glory of our Lord & Saviour,"[9] and the letters of this period exhibit an intense reading of the

Bible. His renewed absorption in the life of Jesus led him to claim that he had regained faith in Divine Providence. On August 16 he wrote, "I must now express to you my conviction that all is come from the spiritual World for Good, & not for Evil,"[10] and on December 11, 1805, he described himself as one "whose Happiness is Secure in Jesus our Lord," adding "I throw myself & all that I have on our Saviour's Divine Providence."[11]

Blake's Christocentrism in these years can be observed not only in the presumed late revisions of *Vala or the Four Zoas* but also in the biblical watercolor drawings he continued to produce in relatively large numbers for Thomas Butts. Blake's first commission from Butts came in 1799 for a set of fifty small biblical paintings in his new tempera technique (Butlin nos. 667–71). They were meant to be small "cabinet pictures," and though many of them are lost, enough have survived to show that they constituted originally a biblical cycle on traditional lines with Old Testament subjects typologically related to those from the New Testament.[12] It is possible even that they were designed for a specific architectural setting, for later, about 1810, Butts bought a group of four or possibly five much larger canvasses, the subjects of which suggest they might have been intended to hang in relation to the earlier tempera series. We are unlikely ever to know whether the hanging scheme in Butts's house was carefully considered, but compositional parallels between Old and New Testament subjects do suggest that it might have been.

Before Blake left for Felpham in September 1800 he must have finished the first tempera series to Butts's satisfaction and, as the date of 1800 on the watercolor drawing of *The Soldiers Casting Lots for Christ's Garment* (Fitzwilliam Museum; Butlin no. 495) confirms, he had already begun to make a series of biblical watercolor drawings for Butts. The accounts between Butts and Blake show that Blake had little time to work on these at Felpham.[13] In one case he had begun a watercolor drawing before he left but had only just finished it before he returned to London on September 19, 1803.[14] After his return he must have worked hard on them, for by 1806 Blake had produced at least seventy biblical scenes for Butts, who seems to have been prepared to pay Blake a guinea for every one that he completed.[15] These watercolors are now widely scattered, a few are certainly lost, and many have suffered from fading. Only a small number are dated, but Butlin's work on Blake's stylistic development has made it possible to date them fairly accurately within a year or so.[16] Uncertainty must remain in many cases because we know that Blake was in the habit of picking up and leaving his designs for indefinite periods. Even so, with the help of the few that are dated, certain groups can be assigned to 1800 and a little later; 1803, when a number are dated and specific stylistic features can be observed; and 1805, when a more emphatic use of outline enters Blake's method. Though these dates are imprecise, they are enough to suggest the order in which Blake treated certain subjects. First of all the possibility, already suggested elsewhere,[17] that Butts might have bought the watercolor drawings in order to extra-illustrate a large Bible would seem to be confirmed by the fact that by 1803 most of the earlier books of the Old Testament were represented by one watercolor only, which could have been inserted as a frontispiece to each book.[18] By this date there was only one for *Genesis (The Angel of the Divine Presence Clothing Adam and Eve*, Butlin no. 436, dated 1803), and there are single illustrations in the 1800–1803 group for *Exodus (Moses and the Burning Bush*, Butlin no. 441); *Leviticus (The Blasphemer*, Butlin no. 446); *Numbers (Moses Erecting the Brazen Serpent*, Butlin no. 447); *Deuteronomy (God Writing on Tables of the Covenant*, Butlin no. 448); *Judges (The Sacrifice of Jephthah's Daughter*, dated 1803, Butlin no. 452); *Ruth (Ruth, the Dutiful Daughter-in-law*, dated 1803, Butlin no. 456). For *I Samuel* there is the *Ghost of Samuel Appearing to Saul* of around 1800 (Butlin no. 450), for *II Samuel, David Pardoning Absalom*, 1800–1803 (Butlin no. 459), and for *Kings, Jeroboam and the Man of God* (Butlin no. 460); *Job (Job Confessing His Presumption*, Butlin no. 461) and *Psalms (Mercy and Truth Are Met Together*, Butlin no. 463) are each represented by one drawing. The biblical books illustrated by Blake make an interesting comparison with the list of biblical books mentioned in *Jerusalem*, plate 48, as written on the canopy of Albion's tomb erected in His mercy by Jesus. This "Spiritual Verse, order'd & measur'd" consists of the "Five books of the Decalogue," by which Blake clearly means the Pentateuch or first five books of the Bible: "the books of Joshua & Judges, / Samuel, a double-book, & Kings, a double book, the Psalms & Prophets, / The Four-fold Gospel, and the Revelations everlasting."[19] Of the Old Testament books as far as *Kings* only Joshua is not represented; *Psalms and Proverbs* are represented, and *Isaac* and *Ezekiel*, added probably as late as 1805. The one book of the Old Testament represented by a watercolor but not on Albion's tomb is in fact the *Book of Job*. If we look at the New Testament watercolors which can be dated 1800–1803, then certainly all four Gospels are represented, and at least two or three for the *Book of Revelation* were evidently completed by 1803. This suggests that the first group of watercolor drawings were dictated by some idea of illustrating what Blake considered to be the essential spiritual books of the Bible.

The dating proposed for this first scheme suggests that he was still working on it on his return to London in September 1803. It is likely that some time after this date the scheme was either regarded as satisfactorily completed or tactfully abandoned, and a further scheme was embarked on for an extensive life of Christ series. We can identify thirty-two watercolor drawings depicting Christ by 1805, including those done in 1800–1803, and excluding those illustrating Acts and the Life of the Virgin. It is possible to isolate within the larger series some groups, possibly made up of works from different dates. These are: the Passion of Christ, a less well-defined set of the Ministry of Christ, and a few of the Infancy of Christ. The Passion series is distinctive in its compositional coherence:[20] the architectural background and the sombre coloring creates a tragic mood throughout the surviving twelve designs. In one notable case Blake has moved beyond the confines of the New Testament by bringing in a subject, *Christ in the Sepulchre*, which is adapted from a text in *Exodus* and here made a prophecy of the Passion.[21] The Old Testament watercolors which can be dated around 1805 reveal some concentration upon Moses, with four watercolor drawings dealing with his life which can be added to *Moses and the Burning Bush* and *The Blasphemer*, the latter being an example of the vengeful Mosaic law (both are from around 1800). This probably reflects Moses' centrality in the traditional conception of the Synagogue rather than that Blake was contemplating separate series.

Blake's first set of *Job* designs must have been made at a time when he was still working on other biblical watercolor drawings for Butts, but it does not fit readily into the sequence already established. The Butts watercolor drawings are smaller in size and the story of Job is taken beyond the Old Testament, for he ultimately achieves redemption through Christ. A central theme of the *Job* series is the ability of pre-Christian man—a state shared by all who have not found Christ in any age—to achieve Christian redemption through vision. The role of Christ as true God in the Job series reflects Blake's concentration on Him in the watercolor drawings of a similar date. But the elevation of Job into a Universal man who reenacts in his own person the Fall and Redemption of mankind suggests that the *Job* designs belonged initially more to the world of Blake's late prophetic books. The powerful sense of spiritual renewal in Blake's letters of the period from 1802 to 1806, expressed equally strongly in the prophecies of this period, *Vala or the Four Zoas, Milton*, and *Jerusalem*, led to major transformations in his account of the history of the human spirit. It has been plausibly argued by Andrew Lincoln[22] that in the course of revising *Vala or the Four Zoas* Blake's new conception of Christ in effect broke the mould of the completed poem *Vala* and led to the late revisions which were eventually abandoned after his return from Felpham. The merciful Christ is conspicuous in those passages which are most likely to have been interpolated in the later revisions. We can also see in these later revisions other new conceptions beginning to emerge which were to achieve a more realised form in *Jerusalem*, for example the geographical identification of the lands of the Old Testament with mythological Britain; on page 19 "Mount Gilead" is deleted and "High Snowden" inserted in its place, and on page 21 "Beth Peor" is replaced by "Conway's Vale."[23] Furthermore, a temporal connection is made explicit, though this was implicit earlier in Blake's thought, between what he saw as the dominant rationalist ideology of contemporary Britain and the legalism of the Old Testament. Babylon is no longer just identified with London but with Natural Religion: as he wrote in a letter to Butts on November 22, 1802, "so now anew began Babylon again in Infancy, Calld Natural Religion."[24] The Fourfold Vision, described by Blake in the same letter, has now been clarified by the identification of the state of Eden as the higher, active Christian Paradise in contrast to Beulah, a passive state of enjoyment, and also, at the lower end, to the state of ultimate despair or Ulro.[25]

It is reasonably certain that by 1807 about sixty plates of *Jerusalem's* final total of one hundred had been completed and that the main elements of the structure and myth were in place by then.[26] A close parallel between the character of Albion, the archetype of mankind, and Job has often been observed, and Lindberg has even claimed that the *Job* illustrations are "the acts of Albion applied to a patriarch of about 1200 B.C."[27] Albion's sufferings in his fallen state can also be seen as reflecting the biblical Job's: he is at all times surrounded by those who lament his state or accuse him. Both Blake's Job and Albion enter into alienation and despair, until they perceive the mercy of Christ and are redeemed. Albion is both "Ancient Man" and national archetype, and therefore the Britain of mythological times and Blake's day; this must also be true of Job, whose limited perceptions in the earlier designs in the series draw together Blake's ideas of the "Old Dispensation" (the montheism of the Old Testament) and the Natural Religion of the eighteenth century in the worship of a legalistic vengeful God.

It is impossible to be sure whether the creation of Albion as the Ancient Man preceded or followed Blake's conception of Job. It is safest to assume that they both emerged at approximately the same time from Blake's reflections upon the idea of an archetypal man. However, despite the broad scheme of Fall and Redemption which Blake's *Job* designs and *Jerusalem* have in common, the relationship between them is not as straightforward as that might imply. In the first place *Jerusalem* does not have a plot which moves forward inexorably toward Redemption: on the contrary, its structure is complex and, as has often been observed, does not correspond to the division into four equal-sized chapters which make up its one hundred plates. Paley, following Henry James's description of *War and Peace,* describes it as a "large loose baggy monster," noting that the story is essentially synchronous; certain events recur again and again at different points in the text and actions are interrupted and taken up again later.[28] The account of the redemption of man occupies only 4 plates, 95–99, the overwhelming majority of the book being devoted to Albion in his fallen state from which he arises only toward the end of the last chapter.[29] The Job illustrations are clearly not conceived with such thematic expansiveness as *Jerusalem,* and the scenes of Redemption roughly balance in number those which pertain to the Fallen world; yet it would be misleading to see the *Job* illustrations as containing only a continuous narrative in which each event or image follows inexorably from the previous one as in Hogarth's *Progresses.* Pictorial parallels between plates can be observed, and the designs fall into discrete groups which in most cases do not advance the plot but rather comment on Job's state of mind. It is probably correct to see the first plate of *Job and His Family* not only as a prelude to the Fall but as representing Job's state of Error, which is also explored in the subsequent scenes of the Fallen world. Similar observations may also be made about the redemptive designs: the final design of *Job and His Wife Restored to Prosperity,* which balances the first scene, is not only the culmination of the process of Job's redemption but also a manifestation of it. As Blake tells us in *A Vision of a Last Judgment,* "Whenever any Individual Rejects Error & Embraces Truth, a Last judgment passes upon that Individual."[30] At the moment Job sees Christ he has entered the redeemed state, one aspect of which is represented by the rapturous and musical praise of God in the final scene.

Certain images in the Fallen state in fact have explicit counterparts in redemption; Job's charity to the beggar in design 5 is balanced by design 19, which shows him in receipt of charity, and it is interesting that Blake later considered making the latter scene balance the former more precisely by a similarly vertical composition in which Christ replaces Jehovah and Satan.[31] Furthermore, most of the designs seem to fall into thematic groups: designs 2–6 reveal the domination of Job's mind by Satan, while 7–10 show Job in the grip of the comforters. And yet it is clear from *Jerusalem* that the state of Satan does not precede the era of the comforters but is coeval with it: the worship of a Satanic God creates a world in which earthly accusers can flourish. Designs 11–13 show the process by which Job comes to see Christ while the following three designs explicate the true nature of the world. The final three, if we again except the additional designs 17 and 20, may all act as counterparts to the first designs in the series; this is obviously so with 19 and 21 and may also apply to design 17, which seems to oppose forgiveness to the comforters' accusation in plate 10. We have then, not as so many commentators have assumed, just a simple narrative leading from Fall to Redemption, but a structure that allows for several levels of interpretation.

Jerusalem combines two central myths, of Humanity and Prophecy:[32] the former is represented by Albion and the latter by Los the prophetic poet. How far does the story of Job in Blake's illustrations correspond to the myth of Humanity in *Jerusalem?* This myth rests itself upon an anterior myth which relates the circumstances of the division of Albion into the Fallen state he has reached when the poem opens. This anterior myth is a sexual one, and Albion's Fallen state is described as one of sexual alienation expressed in guilt and shame.[33] This alienation governs Albion's shifting relationship with the females Vala, who stands for nature, and Jerusalem, who is redemption. In the *Job* designs the most important female presence is Job's wife, who accompanies him throughout. In the first plate she appears to be in total harmony with Job, though her gesture of prayer differentiates her slightly from her husband, who holds the prayer book. In plate 4, however, when disaster is announced, Job looks heavenward submissively while Job's wife wrings her hands in misery above her head. In the following plate, she is submissive and encouraging of Job's conventional charity, but when he is smote with sore boils by Satan she laments abjectly over him. This plate is particularly significant because the image closely resembles a number of those in the lower margins of *Jerusalem*; in particular plate 19 in which the giant Albion is mourned by Jerusalem and Vala, who offer him respectively a vision of innocence and a reminder of his shame, which has brought him to the Fallen state.[34] Albion in his reply in plate 21 compares himself implicitly to Job himself:

> *The disease of Shame covers me from head to feet. I have no hope.*
> *Every boil upon my body is a separate & deadly Sin.*
> *Doubt first assail'd me, then Shame took possession of me.*
> *Shame divides Families, Shame hath divided Albion in sunder.*
> *First fled my Sons & then my Daughters, then my Wild Animations*
> *My Cattle next, last ev'n the Dog of my Gate; the Forests fled,*
> *The Corn-fields & the breathing Gardens outside separated*
> *The Sea; the Stars: the Sun: the Moon: driv'n forth by my disease*[35]

If Albion's boils are the consequence of sexual shame, then the same must also apply on one level of interpretation to Job, whose wife's despair parallels that of Jerusalem and Vala and whose alienation from Job is made even more explicit in the designs which precede Job's redemption. In design 7 her gesture of horror parallels that of the three comforters, and in plate 8 she is united with them completely in their lamentations and accusations. Her separation from them, however, quickly becomes apparent in the redemptive designs; in design 13 she is at one with Job before God in the whirlwind while the comforters prostrate themselves as if before an idol. She remains united with Job through plates 14–16, but it should be noted that in design 18, like the comforters, she is in need of Job's forgiveness, for she also supplicates before the altar. In the final scene she is, of course, fully restored to him and plays upon a musical instrument with Job and their new family.

If Job's wife broadly reflects the sexual themes of *Jerusalem*, we might also expect Job's sons and daughters to parallel the actions of the sons and daughters of Albion. Albion's role in relation to his sons is a complex one, for he begins as a figure of authority but remains throughout most of Jerusalem as their victim.[36] Job in the first three designs certainly appears to be dominant over his sons; he leads them in conventional prayer, and in design 3—insofar as Satan represents Job's mental state—he acts as avenger upon both his sons and daughters, whose wine cups and tambourine are evidence of their licentiousness. The sons and daughters do not appear collectively again, except insofar as they are regenerated as Job's second family, and the daughters alone appear again only in design 20, which does not, of course, belong with the original 19 Butts watercolor designs. It is possible that by analogy with *Jerusalem* Job's comforters themselves are in a sense meant to be his sons, and thus would correspond with the threefold form in which Albion's accusers often appear in *Jerusalem*. They are sometimes identified there as Hand, Hyle, and Coban, but in plate 51 Vala, Hyle, and Skofeld are shown; their threefold nature finds an analogy in Socrates' accusers Anytus, Melitus, and Lycon depicted on plate 93, who are also the triumvirate of Bacon, Locke and Newton. Job's accusers in design 10 might be seen therefore to represent the association between Job's shame and the mental tyranny he imposes upon himself and others, but the beginning of his redemption may be hinted at in this design in his apparent rejection of their accusations.

Job has three daughters in both the fallen and the redeemed state, but they do not appear to play a significant role in the Butts series, though they do appear in the first, second, and final designs. At first sight it would also appear that the myth in *Jerusalem* of prophecy, embodied in the figure of Los, also plays a relatively small part. However, though a true prophet is evidently only brought to the fore in one design, no. 12, his intervention is a crucial one. The appearance of Elihu and his words to Job are the direct prelude to Christ's appearance to Job in the whirlwind. Elihu is the second person to make a prophetic statement to Job; he is preceded in this on plate 9 by Eliphaz, one of the three comforters, who in recounting his dream reiterates the justice of Job's punishment and reaffirms his guilt. Eliphaz is therefore a type of false prophet whose role in *Jerusalem* is taken by Hand, the "Reasoning Spectre." Elihu, on the other hand, appears, as Lindberg has pointed out, in the attitude of Raphael's St. Paul preaching[37] and is represented as a wrathful prophet whose role is to rouse the soul of Job to know its own true state. The poet in *Milton, a Poem* is divided between the mild and wrathful attitudes called by Blake respectively Palambron and Rintrah; here we have a Rintrah-like figure who rages against Job's mechanistic universe. It is left, however, not to Elihu but to Christ to explain the story of the universe in designs 14–16.

In *Jerusalem* Los is tormented by his Spectre, who represents his reasoning self and the conventional materialism of Blake's contemporaries. He is divided from his Emanation, Enitharmon, who also seeks to thwart his prophetic destiny. The Spectre is part of Los's consciousness and also has the form of Jehovah of the Old Testament: the vision of a vengeful God is brought into being as an aspect of Los's own division.[38] The connection between Los's Spectre and Job's vision of God in his fallen state becomes explicit in Jerusalem plate 91, where the Spectre forms Leviathan and Behemoth. Job's Satan is not a counter-principle to the Jehovah who presides over the fallen world but his active existence in his relations with fallen humanity. In terms of the myth of humanity in *Jerusalem*, Job is in a state of Satan or Error expressed in his belief that God is inherently vengeful. Satan's accusation of Job is, therefore, an aspect of Job's state of spiritual sleep and Error, in which he worships the "god of this world" who is Satan. In *Jerusalem* Satan is explicitly associated with all periods of human history, and Job's error in worshipping Jehovah can be applied equally to Blake's own contemporaries, the Deists who are addressed at the beginning of Chapter 3 of *Jerusalem*: "Every Religion that Preaches Vengeance for Sin is the Religion of the Enemy & Avenger and not of the Forgiver of Sin, and their God is Satan . . . Deism, is the Worship of the God of this World."[39] The punishments of Job are then the acts of Satan and can be associated with other horrors including those inflicted upon the Egyptians by Moses, the Civil War, Plague and Fire visited upon London in the seventeenth century, and the apocalyptic wrath which will be unleashed in the Last Days as prophesied in the Book of Revelation.

The vengeful image of God the Father appears in *Jerusalem* as the creation of the Spectre, and the Spectre's description in plate 10 precisely conforms to Job's experience of him: "For he is Righteous, he is not a Being of Pity & Compassion, / He cannot feel Distress, he feeds on Sacrifice & Offering, / Delighting in cries & tears & clothed in holiness & solitude";[40] He is an "impersonal God" whose character is a consequence of Job's belief that God is indeed impersonal. Job seems to discover the identity of Satan and Jehovah in design 11 where he is tormented by a curiously merged figure of the two which combines white-bearded gravity with a cloven hoof and enfolding serpent. This realization enables Job to see his mistake in separating the vengefulness of Satan from the majesty of Jehovah and helps him at last to be receptive to the voice of prophecy. It should be noted that while Satan becomes Los's Spectre in *Jerusalem* and acts as the voice of reason attempting to persuade Los to give up prophecy, in the *Job* designs this Spectral role is attached to Job, the archetype of humanity.

Job's vision of a vengeful Jehovah is a function of his Fallen state, in which Jehovah is separated from man's redemptive portion or Christ. However, in the redemptive state he is united with his son whose physiognomy he shares, as does Job: the presiding deity Job worships is Christ, but Christ now united with His father whose vengeful aspect has been shed. Though in one sense it would be correct to say that Job progresses from the worship of Jehovah to the worship of Christ, in another sense they are one God transformed by Job's perceptions from a vengeful to a merciful one. Furthermore, in *Jerusalem* as in other late writings, Jehovah appears as a figure of forgiveness, quite distinct from the cruel Urizen of the prophecies of the 1790s, whose covenant is now expressed in "Forgiveness of Sins which is Self Annihilation" (plate 98). Job's redemption in Blake's designs follows the speech of Elihu when God-as-Christ appears to him in a whirlwind (design 13). Job's recognition of Him as the Divine Humanity and the human imagination is essential to redemption; but He does not preside in His own person over the last four designs of Job's redemptive phase, for having received Divine revelation and knowledge, Job is now at one with Christ in the acts which follow that reception. In the Butts series, Job enters into the state of forgiveness, the central tenet of Christ's new Dispensation (as opposed to the Old Dispensation), by offering it to the friends who had tormented him and sought to lead him into false paths (design 18). Satan, however, has already been cast out, for he is not an individual but a State: "Satan is the state of Death & not a Human existence," and it is only by distinguishing the States from "the Eternal Human / That walks about among the stones of fire in bliss & woe / Alternate" that man can reach the "Forgiveness of Enemies."[41]

John Linnell first saw the *Job* watercolor drawings at Butts's house in 1821.[42] Blake initially appeared to have had little interest in revising them and agreed to let Linnell make tracings of them in Blake's company.[43] After Linnell had traced most of them Blake took over the task himself and completely redrew and colored the final designs, probably adding two new designs which correspond to plates 17 and 20 and substantially altering design 18.[44] These additions balanced the set more evenly between Job's Fall and Redemption, and the number of designs—now 21—would have seemed more regular than the previous 19. This process of adjustment may be compared with Blake's work on *Jerusalem* around this time, which involved adding and occasionally altering plates to order the work into a scheme of one hundred plates made up of four evenly balanced chapters of twenty-five plates each. Though Blake's thought does not appear to have changed substantially between around 1804 and 1807, when the Butts *Job* designs were conceived, and the 1820s, some shifts of emphasis can be discerned in the few writings from the last years. Certain addition of two designs to the redemptive scenes would seem to suggest not only an increasing concentration upon the redeemed state in the 1820s but also a dogmatic insistence upon the absolute incompatibility of world and spirit which can be observed in the *Laocoön* print of around 1820–22.[45] The interpolated design for plate 17, which almost certainly makes its first appearance in the Linnell set, shows God as Christ blessing Job and his wife, whose entry into His light is strongly contrasted with the still cast-out comforters. Their despairing postures and their willful refusal to see the light of Christ shows that they are still in Error, for they have yet to receive forgiveness. At this stage Job has accepted Christ but has not *become* Christ, as he will in the next design when the comforters join him in the sacrifice.

The design for plate 20 of *Job and His Daughters* makes its first appearance in the context of the series in the Linnell set, though the composition can be found in a painting of 1799–1800 in the Butts tempera series (Butlin no. 394), where the scene is set in a small room. The Linnell version is curiously ambiguous: it seems to be set in a small room with designs on the back wall but there are also sheep in the foreground. It is impossible now to trace the exact sequence of Blake's changes of mind: the Butts watercolor drawing and a pencil drawing (Butlin no. 556) are set outdoors but in the final engraving returned to an indoor scene. The indecision is hard to explain but may be due, like the proposed change to design 19, to a desire for visual compatibility with the other scenes which are all set outdoors, even though it is clear in design 4, for example, that Job and his wife are intended to be seen in their own house. Even so the essential idea remains the same in all versions: Job recounts the story of his life by means of visual images, which either float in the sky or form part of a circular frieze of either paintings or bas-reliefs within a room or sanctuary. The scene is clearly one of Edenic discourse which transcends earthly conversation by uniting all the senses. Such conversation is described as "Visionary forms dramatic" in plate 98 of *Jerusalem*,[46] and design 20 should be seen with the final design of *Job and His Family Restored to Prosperity* as expressing forms of discourse which unite in exultation poetry, architecture, painting or sculpture, music and song, and perhaps even dance.

Plate 98 of *Jerusalem* appears to belong to the large group of plates completed before 1807, so the idea of the transcendent unity of the arts was already in Blake's mind before the 1820s. Nor is there anything in the interpolated design no. 17 which is incompatible with his thought before 1810 or so. However, if one takes into account the margins added to the engraved plates for the first time between 1823 and 1825, including quotations from the Bible and supplementary designs, then a much greater emphasis upon the role of art in the process of redemption can be observed. The idea that Jesus was synonymous with the artistic imagination had been expressed as early as 1805—"The Mocker of Art is the Mocker of Jesus"[47]—but there is a greater insistence observable in the 1820s on the absolute identity of art with prayer and true Christianity, especially in the *Laocoön* print.

In plate 18 of the engraved series, the prayer of forgiveness is associated in the margin with a burin, palette, and brushes, drawing together the notion of art with prayer but also associating with the act of forgiveness Blake's own creation of the *Job* illustrations. The final plate also expresses the centrality of art, but by adding to the series plate 20 and the marginal additions to plate 18 the redeemed state of mankind is made as much a union of art and life as of man and Christ.

Though problems remain in deciphering the marginal designs, they employ in most cases the symbolic language Blake established in his earlier illuminated books. The Fallen state is associated with images of the pastoral paradise in plates 2 and 3, and of the natural world, often with sinister connotations of decay and destruction in other plates. The margins of the scenes of Redemption have, as one might expect, images associated with Christ and the Second Coming like the vine and wheat. Yet the most substantial change between the watercolor drawings and the final engravings is one which, as Robert Essick observes,[48] transcends the distinction between technique and imagery. In the *Job* engravings light plays a central role in defining the contrast between the worlds of Fall and Redemption. The rhythm of the engraved lines suggests with great subtlety the more exalted light of Redemption and gives greater precision to the diurnal cycle which runs through the work from beginning to end. It is this new sensitivity to natural and spiritual light, observable in his work of the 1820s, which gives them the autumnal quality so often remarked upon by commentators, and serves to disguise the complexity of the work's genesis. The *Job* engravings stand out from almost all Blake's work in their completeness and finish, yet, as we have seen, this happy result was by no means inherent in the original conception. Were it not for the intervention of John Linnell they would have remained another venture which did not reach its full potential in Blake's most fertile period of invention.

This essay is adapted and reprinted, with permission from the author, from his introduction to *William Blake's Illustrations of the Book of Job*, first published by The William Blake Trust in 1987.

Notes

1. Gilchrist 1863, pp. 282–3. Gilchrist seems to date the Butts series as late as 1822.
2. Butlin (1981) dates the Butts series to about 1805–6. Lindberg (1973) had suggested about 1810 and Bindman (1977b), 1805–10.
3. Butlin (1981, p. 411) suggests a date of about 1821–27 for the two drawings and notes that they "differ in style and technique from the rest and are both on different paper." The two drawings also show the intervention of another hand, particularly in the coloring. See note 4.
4. M. Butlin, "Cataloguing William Blake," in Essick and Pearce 1978, pp. 85-88.
5. See also Bindman 1977b, pp. 186–92. (Note: Hereafter, "Butlin no." refers to the catalog numbers in Butlin 1981.)
6. For the dating of these works I have depended heavily on Bentley 1978.
7. Lincoln 1978, pp. 115–33.
8. Keynes 1980, no. 39.
9. Ibid., no. 45.
10. Ibid., no. 49.
11. Ibid., no. 94.
12. Bindman 1977b, pp. 118–25.
13. Bentley 1969, pp. 570–71.
14. This is the *Three Maries at the Sepulchre* (Butlin no. 503), which was mentioned as having been no "forwarder" in a letter to Butts of October 2, 1800, but was described as "now on the Stocks" on July 6, 1803, and received by Butts on July 8 or August 20 of that year.
15. Bentley 1969, p. 572.
16. See Butlin 1978, no. 86.
17. Bindman 1982, p. 132.
18. The subjects can be identified from either Blake's own biblical references in the corner of the work, or in some cases from inscriptions in a copperplate hand (probably not Blake's own) on the matt beneath, though many of these have been cut away.
19. Keynes 1966, p. 677.
20. See Butlin 1978, no. 93.
21. Cf. Butlin 1981, no. 500; also *Vala or the Four Zoas* (Keynes 1966, p. 341).
22. Lincoln 1978, p. 125.
23. Bentley 1978, 2: 1103, 1106.
24. Ibid., p. 1250. *Night the Eighth*, p. 111. By "Natural Religion" Blake meant a sort of Deism, which is based on the idea that moral ideas can be derived from sense perception. Poetic Genius, on the other hand, was for Blake universal, and could be found in Christ.
25. Lincoln 1978, p. 122.
26. Bentley 1978, 1: 727-8.
27. Lindberg 1973, p. 72.
28. Paley 1983, pp. 283-90.
29. Paley (ibid., p. 289) claims that "*Jerusalem* is a work virtually all middle."
30. Bentley 1978, 1: 613.
31. See fascicule 20 of Bindman 1987a.
32. Paley 1983, p. 234.
33. Ibid., pp. 167-78.
34. See also plate 9.
35. *Jerusalem*, pl. 21; Bentley 1978, 1:643.
36. Paley 1983, pp. 212-21.
37. In the *Blinding of Elymas* cartoon. Lindberg 1973, p. 117.
38. Paley 1983, pp. 244-5.
39. Bentley 1978, 1: 682.
40. Ibid., p. 630.
41. Ibid., p. 680.
42. Bindman 1987a, p. 104.
43. Ibid.
44. Butlin 1981, p. 411.
45. Bentley 1978, 1: 775.
46. Ibid., p. 746.
47. Keynes 1980, no. 94.
48. Bindman 1987a, pp. 38 ff.

SELECTED BIBLIOGRAPHY

Ackroyd, Peter. 1996. *Blake.* New York.

Bentley, G. E., Jr. 1969. *Blake Records.* Oxford.

——. 1971. "Blake's Job Copperplates." *The Library Transactions of the Bibliographical Society 26* (September): 231-41.

——. 1975. *William Blake: The Critical Heritage.* London.

——. 1977. *Blake Books.* Oxford.

——. 1978. *William Blake's Writings.* 2 vols. Oxford and New York.

Bindman, D., ed. 1970. *William Blake: Catalogue of the Collection in the Fitzwilliam Museum.* Cambridge, Eng.

——. 1974. "Blake's Job". *Times Literary Supplement,* March 14, 1974, p. 341.

——. 1977a. Review of *William Blake's Illustrations to the Book of Job,* by Bo Lindberg. *Burlington Magazine* 119: 451-2.

——. 1977b. *Blake as an Artist.* Oxford and New York.

——, assisted by D. Toomey. 1978. *The Complete Graphic Works of William Blake.* London.

——. 1982. *William Blake: His Art and Times.* Catalogue of an exhibition at Yale Center for British Art, New Haven, and Art Gallery of Ontario, Toronto.

——, ed. 1987a. *Blake's Illustrations of the Book of Job.* London.

——. 1987b. *Colour Versions of William Blake's Book of Job Designs.* 3 vols. London.

Binyon, L. 1926. *The Engraved Designs of William Blake.*

——, and G. L. Keynes. 1935. *Illustrations of the Book of Job... being all the water-color designs, pencil drawings and engravings, reproduced in facsimile.* New York.

Blake, W. 1918. *Catalogue of the John Linnell Collection of Highly Important Works by William Blake obtained direct from the Artist.* Christie's, London, March 15, 1918.

Blunt, Anthony. 1959. *The Art of William Blake.* London and New York.

Butlin, M. 1975. Review of *William Blake's Illustrations of the Book of Job,* by Bo Lindberg. *Art Bulletin* 57: 295-6.

——. 1978. *William Blake, Catalogue of an Exhibition at the Tate Gallery, March–May,* 1978. London.

——. 1981. *The Paintings and Drawings of William Blake. Catalogue of Water Colour Drawings, Painted Drawings and Wood Blocks by William Blake.* Christie's, London, December 2, 1938.

Damon, S. Foster. 1966. *Blake's Job: William Blake's Illustrations of the Book of Job.* Providence.

——. 1965, 1971. *A Blake Dictionary: The Ideas and Symbols of William Blake.* New York.

Essick, R. 1976. Review of *William Blake's Illustrations of the Book of Job,* by Bo Lindberg. *Studies in Romanticism* 15: 469-72.

——. 1980. *William Blake, Printmaker.* Providence.

——. 1983. "John Linnell, William Blake, and the Printmaker's Craft." *Huntington Library Quarterly* 46: 18-32. San Marino, Calif.

——, and Pearce, D., eds. 1978. *Blake and His Time.* London.

Frye, N. 1969. "Blake's Reading of the *Book of Job.*" In *William Blake: Essays for S. Foster Damon,* ed. Alvin H. Rosenfeld, pp. 221-34. Providence.

Gilchrist, A. 1863. *Life of William Blake.* 2 vols. London.

Grant, J. 1974. "Blake's Illustrations of the *Book of Job.*" *Times Literary Supplement,* March 14, 1974, pp. 271-2.

Hamblen, E. 1939. *The Book of Job Interpreted.* New York.

Hofer, P. 1937. *Illustrations of the Book of Job by William Blake from the original 'New Zealand' set reproduced in facsimile.* New York.

Hoover, S. 1973. "William Blake in the Wilderness: A Closer Look at His Reputation, 1827–1853." In *Essays in Honour of Sir Geoffrey Keynes,* ed. Morton D. Paley and Michael Phillips, pp. 310–48. Oxford.

Keynes, G. L. 1943. "New Blake Documents: History of the Job Engravings." *Times Literary Supplement,* January 9, 1943, p. 24.

——, and E. Wolf. 1953. *William Blake's Illuminated Books: A Census.* New York.

——. *Blake Studies: Essays on His Life and Work,* 2nd ed. First published 1949. Oxford.

——, ed. 1966. *Blake: The Complete Writings with variant readings.* First published 1957, London. Reprint: Oxford.

——, ed. 1980. *Letters of William Blake.* First published 1956; rev. ed. 1968. Oxford.

Kiralis, K. 1975. Review of *Blake's Job: A Commentary,* by Andrew Wright. *Blake Studies* 7: 182-6.

LaBelle, J. 1973. "Words Graven with an Iron Pen: The Marginal Texts in Blake's Job." In *The Visionary Hand: Essays for the Study of William Blake's Art and Aesthetics,* ed. Robert Essick, pp. 527-50. Los Angeles.

Lemaitre, H. 1953. "Les Illustrations pour le Livre de Job par William Blake." Unpublished Ph.D. thesis, University of Paris.

Lincoln, Andrew. 1978. "The revision of the Seventh and Eighth Nights of *The Four Zoas.*" *Blake Illustrated Quarterly* 12, no. 2: 115–33.

Lindberg, B. 1973. *William Blake's Illustrations to the Book of Job.* Abo, Finland.

Lister, Raymond, 1986. *The Paintings of William Blake.* Cambridge, Eng.

Morley, Edith J., ed. 1938. *Henry Crabb Robinson on Books and Their Writers.* 3 vols. London.

Nelms, B. 1970. "Text and Design in Illustrations of the *Book of Job.*" In Blake's *Visionary Forms Dramatic,* ed. David V. Erdman and John E. Grant. Princeton.

Noon, Patrick. 1997. *"The Human Form Divine," William Blake from the Paul Mellon Collection.* New Haven.

Paley, M.D. 1983. *The Continuing City: William Blake's Jerusalem.* Oxford.

Raine, K. 1969. *Blake and Tradition.* 2 vols. London.

——. 1982. *The Human Face of God: William Blake and the Book of Job.* London.

Redgrave, S. 1874. *A Dictionary of Artists of the English School.* London.

Russell, A. G. B. 1912. *The Engravings of William Blake.* London.

Safire, William. 1992. *The First Dissident: The Book of Job in Today's Politics.* New York.

Spencer, J. 1975. "Review of William Blake's Illustrations to the Book of Job, by Bo Lindberg." *Blake Studies* 6: 197–201.

Story, A. 1892. *The Life of John Linnell.* 2 vols. 1892. London.

Viscomi, Joseph. 1983. *The Art of William Blake's Iluminated Prints.* Manchester, England.

——. 1983. *Blake and the Idea of the Book.* Princeton.

Wicksteed, J. 1924. *Blake's Vision of the Book of Job.* Rev. and enlarged ed. Originally published 1910, London.

——. 1971. *Blake's Vision of the Book of Job.* New York.

Wilson, M. 1971. *The Life of William Blake,* a new edition edited by Geoffrey Keynes. Previously published 1927, 1932, 1948.

Wolf, E. 1943. "The Blake-Linnell Accounts in the Library of Yale University." *Papers of the Bibliographical Society of America* 37: 1-22.

Wright, A. 1972. *Blake's Job: A Commentary.* Oxford.

INDEX

INDEX OF NAMES

INDEX OF WORKS

Book of Job Designs

Other Works by Blake

**Initials refer to the owners of Blake's Job designs:* VM = Virginia Museum of Fine Arts; FM = Fitzwilliam Museum, Cambridge, England; PM = Pierpont Morgan Library, New York; YC = Yale Center for British Art, New Haven. Italicized numbers refer to pages with illustrations.